Also by Le Tat Dieu

Letters to Bloomington, Illinois

Some Words of Advice to the Commander-in-Chief

What you Don't Know Might Hurt your Country

Le Tat Dieu

Edited by James Banerian

iUNIVERSE, INC.
NEW YORK   BLOOMINGTON

Some Words of Advice to the Commander-in-Chief

iUniverse books may be ordered through booksellers or by contacting:

iUniverse
1663 Liberty Drive
Bloomington, IN 47403
www.iuniverse.com
1-800-Authors (1-800-288-4677)

Because of the dynamic nature of the Internet, any Web addresses or links contained in this book may have changed since publication and may no longer be valid.

ISBN: 978-1-4401-5666-3 (sc)
ISBN: 978-1-4401-5667-0 (hc)
ISBN: 978-1-4401-5668-7 (ebk)

Library of Congress Control Number: 2009932492

Printed in the United States of America

iUniverse rev. date: 7/23/2009

Special Thanks

Le Tuan

Brigitte V. Zaki, Dao Le, San Le

Le Quang Hiep

1

When the Disaster Started

Dear Commander-in-Chief,

On August 20, 2003, I wrote in the *Little Saigon magazine* about a decision that undermined the American efforts and good intention in Iraq as follows:

Arriving in Baghdad in May 03, and after only a few days as Iraq's top civil administrator, L Paul Bremer threw his first "country-rebuilding" punch that defied all common sense: He ordered the dissolution of the Iraqi armed forces and several security bodies.

These forces were not temporarily "laid off", but permanently dismissed, because the new King decided that he would create a new police force and a new army for his kingdom.

It was quite obvious that Bremer had little knowledge about the basic thinking and reaction of humankind.

Here are some of the things he either forgot or ignored:

Iraqi soldiers are human being, too, and like Americans and people all over the world they have a need to feed themselves, their spouses, and their children. From out of nowhere comes a guy from abroad who identifies himself as a great liberator yet robs them of the means to earn a living, depriving their families of food, clothing and shelter. Naturally, they will become angry, as would any ordinary people who find themselves in the same situation. Many may even choose violence to protect their survival.

Now an American who is fired unjustly (or believes he is being unjustly fired, treated unfairly, etc.) may become dangerous. Some come back to the workplace with a gun. (In the latest incident on Aug. 27, 03 in Chicago, the fourth in the U.S. this year, 7 lives were lost.) The Iraqis, no matter how naïve, timid, uneducated, or terrified by America's power, are people, too. And people who are oppressed and desperate can easily become dangerous.

Ambassador Bremer, in one fell swoop, fired the entire Iraqi armed forces and several security bodies, sacking about a half million in staff. All of them have weapons, have been trained to shoot and kill, and have been through several wars that went on for years. Those half million unemployed, angry, and desperate fighters also have families, relatives, and friends who are now also put in that same desperate situation. This would raise the number of people who would likely want to repel the "invaders" to a million. Wow!

Just like magic, in only the few seconds it took for Bremer to sign orders of dissolution, he instantly created another million formidable enemies for American soldiers to deal with. (I say "another" because the invasion itself had brought them quite a few already.)

The result of Bremer's action came quickly.

Thousands of Iraqi officers and soldiers demonstrated, peacefully at first, to protest Bremer's orders, and to request the liberators respect their right to live by paying them a salary. In a deadly moment, U.S. soldiers shot into the crowd, killing two former Iraqi officers and wounding a dozen, explaining that they were returning fire.

In the funeral for the two victims, the crowd no longer asked for salaries or any other favors from the liberator. They shouted a vow of revenge, and death wishes to America.

I don't know how talented Mr. Bremer was to earn the position of representing America and leading the U.S. liberation team in Iraq. But based on his first rebuilding measure, I am afraid that his judgment, knowledge, and intelligence may not even be enough for the position of a human resources manager of a small company in the U.S.

In the U.S., if a human resources manager starts to rebuild his company by firing everybody at once and then filling up all positions with newly hired people, he would put the company in deep trouble. The former employees would sue the employer to the last penny. The more aggressive ones would picket in front of the company with the potential of it exploding into a violent confrontation. If those fired employees were still living *inside* the company (were not deported to… Iran or Jordan) sabotage would occur as frequently as the news that arrives daily on the desk of Mr. Bremer, reporting incidences of U.S. soldiers being ambushed and killed.

Awakened by the deadly conflict caused by his creative rebuilding program, Mr. Bremer tried to initiate damage control. He threw out a new order: The Iraqi armed forces are still being dissolved, no changes. But *the army officers will continue to receive their salaries.*

To save himself from embarrassment, Bremer ordered the Iraqi officers to sign papers vowing to renounce their loyal to Saddam Hussein and his Baath party. This was to show the whole world, and especially Bremer's superiors, that he had initially denied those men their livelihoods because they had failed to sign some very important, precious papers.

Unfortunately, while taking the above corrective measures, Bremer was only half-awake. His mind was only clear on part of the whole picture. He forgot something: the Iraqi soldiers and their families have the same unfortunate habit as the officers; without food, they also feel hungry and need to eat!

By paying only the officers, Bremer's rescue plan did not reach the soldiers and their families, who were poorer and more desperate. The majority of the angry crowd was still in the hole Bremer had dug. What made this man think that his revised plan, which only solved a tiny part of the problem, could satisfy a half of million angry and humiliated fighters?

The crowd refused to calm down, so Bremer began reconsidering his decision to dissolve the armed forces. But then, he changed his mind. He flatly announced: No changes are necessary. He would rebuild for Iraq, in three years time, an army of 40,000, one-tenth the size of the former forces.

The Iraqi soldiers now had a definite decision about their future: Ambassador Bremer had no way for them to work or make a living in the job of their choice. Even if Mr. Bremer were kind enough to build the new armed forces with all re-hired soldiers, only 40,000 would have jobs - 40,000 out of a half million hopeless and desperate men.

On the surface, and despite their doubts about the *"good intentions"* of the Liberator, the Iraqi soldiers seemed to accept their new fate, stopped demonstrating and peacefully disappeared.

But are they really gone, those poor professional fighters? I'll address this question later.

One thing I know for sure: They totally disappeared from the reports of Mr. Bremer - from his press releases and conferences. Actually they had never appeared in any of them. Bremer never pointed his finger to those unemployed Iraqis while identifying the terrorists who are now causing all kinds of trouble in Iraq.

To explain the ambushes, attacks and killings of American soldiers happening almost daily, Bremer and the Secretary of Defense Donald Rumsfeld changed the identity of the culprits. At first, they blamed Saddam, who had released thousands of criminals before the invasion.

They said that those criminals were now committing all kinds of crimes in Iraq, including ambushing and attacking American soldiers and whoever cooperated or worked with the U.S. Then Baath party loyalists and the remnants of Saddam's Fedayeen were accused. The terrorist group al-Taifa al-Mansouri, stationed far away somewhere in Algeria, also made the list of troublemakers. Then Mr. Bremer's intelligence suddenly pointed to Ansar Al Islam as the real culprit of all the recent killings and bombings. But mainly, the Pentagon went with the theory that the Saddam loyalists, who badly wanted to see him back in power, comprised the main evil force in Iraq, and U.S. soldiers were ordered to urgently find Saddam and his two sons. Our military strategists believed that catching or killing them would render those loyalists hopeless and they would give up fighting.

Nowhere in all of these talks, reports, press releases, and interviews do we find mention of the Iraqi soldiers who wanted to kill Americans because Bremer had insulted them and robbed them of their livelihoods. Bremer totally ignored these extremely angry men, denying them even the distinction of being recognized as the *dangerous enemy* of the American soldiers.

If Bremer were the luckiest ambassador on earth, and 90% of the half million Iraqi soldiers were cowards who threw away their weapons and quit fighting immediately after he laid them off, he still would have at least tens of thousands of Iraqis who would quietly choose to kill the occupiers. But these have not been mentioned on his terrorist list!

Is it possible that Bremer is just very naïve, and that he truly believes the Iraqi soldiers are so impressed by the promising model of democracy that they are willing to endure the hardship of life without food?

I don't think so, because the top administrator of Iraq still has his ears to listen to the victims and critics, and his eyes to see the result of his actions.

On the same "day of dissolution", an Iraqi officer told the press: Before attacking Iraq, the U.S. army rained on Iraqi troops leaflets carrying the

American President's message saying that everything will be OK if they do not fight back. Many of us obeyed. Now the American President does not honor his promise and robs us of our livelihood. How will my family live? I won't sit quietly to watch my children die of starvation. I will fight to kick the invaders out of my country!

Although the Iraqi officers received some salary after Bremer's amended order, did this quell the anger and turn the officers into the ambassador's admirers? Here are some of their feelings on that payday as reported by Hamza Hendawi of AP:

They sweated for hours in the searing heat. Many were grim-faced, some resentful, even angry. There was talk of revenge and no hint of gratitude.
...Ghaleb Mattar, a former air defense lieutenant colonel, said delays in paying members of the armed forces have caused families untold hardships. Mattar said it might drive some, including himself, to join the insurgents. "We collected our last salaries in April." he said Thursday, after collecting his money. "If we are to stay that long again without any money, I'll strap myself with explosives and blow myself up in the middle of the Americans."
... "Do you see our humiliation?" said Abu el-Hakim, a colonel in Saddam Hussein's defeated army, as he stood in a long line of fellow officers to collect a one-time $100 payment from U.S. coalition authorities. "These Americans only deserve our rocket-propelled grenades, nothing else," he said, referring to the weapon of choice of Iraqi insurgents attacking U.S. troops...

Those were the true feelings of some of the lucky ones who were *eligible to receive some money!*

Mr. Bremer might dismiss the Iraqi soldiers' and officers' observations, arguing that they were already resistant to any plans from the U.S. But there are people whose wisdom, experience, and leadership skills are harder to ignore, like former Israeli Prime Minister Ehud Barak and Egyptian President Hosni Mubarak, and they have determined that Bremer's action was a big mistake.

During a visit to New York, Barak told the press that the Iraqi police would do a very good job in securing civil society (implying that

Bremer's decision to replace them with U.S. soldiers and new recruits was not a good idea.)

President Mubarak criticized Bremer more directly, saying that the decision to dissolve the Iraqi army and other state jobs was a mistake, which would result in higher unemployment and fuel crime. On July 26, 03, at a meeting with students in Egypt's Mediterranean city of Alexandria, Mubarak remarked: *"[The Iraqi] earns no money. How is he going to live? How is he going to eat? How is he going to dress his children?... Naturally, he's going to work as a criminal, he'll join any gang. He'll become desperate."* (Reuters.)

I believe the Egyptian President was trying to be diplomatic and avoided mentioning the next step, which if revealed, would expose the weakness in the leadership of the U.S. administration and damage the reputation of his ally.

The omitted fact is this: Those unemployed professional fighters would not only become criminals, thieves and robbers... they would also play a major role in ambushing, attacking and killing American soldiers.

Some desperate soldiers might choose robbery as convenient way to make money in an emergency, exactly as the Egyptian president predicted. But the majority, I believe, would wish to retain their dignity, rather than becoming thugs to make a living.

The Iraqi armed forces, well organized, experienced, and comprising almost a half million, does not have to rob and steal to earn money. Just find a noble cause to fight for and everybody, from the privates to the generals, can become heroes. The Iraqi people will offer them money, supplies, material and spiritual assistance. After all there are patriots among the Iraqi people, too.

Talking about noble causes, our president has found a good one for the U.S. Army. By attacking and invading Iraq, our main goal was to get rid of Saddam and eliminate a major threat to America. The cause sounds pure national self interest. But by labeling our soldiers "Liberators" at the last minute, all at once, he made them heroes deserving the admiration of the whole world.

Some Iraqi army leaders might be as smart as Mr. Bush, I'm afraid. They would call themselves the real liberators as they are fighting to liberate the Iraqis from foreign occupiers. Now we know we are the good guys and our president is sincere, but the Iraqis don't necessary think so. Mr. Bremer's decision has convinced millions of Iraqis that the disbanded Iraqi army is the true liberator and the noble cause now belongs to their side.

Bremer told the press that, according to a poll, only 15% of the Iraqi people hate America. The remaining 85% like Americans very much and believe that they will bring prosperity, happiness and democracy to Iraq. If this is true, and all the wealthy Iraqis are on the same side as the 85% who love America and detest the terrorists, would the Iraqi army then be in trouble and go hungry again?

I don't think so. Besides a noble cause, they have another very effective tool to make quick money in a lawless society: violence.

They can compel with force the non-voluntary support of others. In daytime they can cover their faces and set up checkpoints to collect highway fees. At night, they can visit some wealthy families and demand contributions to their cause. Who would dare resist them?

The terrorist organizations in the Middle East, inspired and excited by the chance to kill Americans, would happily send them money, volunteers and weapons. This has caused Mr. Bremer to claim to the media that those foreign militants, the hundreds of Ansar al-Islam members who have entered Iraq to perform terrorist acts, are the real culprits.

He doesn't know (or doesn't want to know) that those militants are only a small group of terrorists who have come to reinforce the bigger one that already exists inside Iraq, the one numbering in the hundreds thousands that Bremer unwittingly created.

So the unemployed Iraqi Army has not disappeared as he had hoped. It has become a mighty power in the dark that rules an important part of Iraq.

Bremer has good reason to make these dangerous and angry Iraqi men invisible to the public. He needs to protect his new throne and the handsome paychecks of the top Occupier.

But by doing so, he has denied the President, the Vice President, the National security Advisor, and the Secretary of Defense, the chance to identify and eliminate the real problem, and begin corrective measures.

The administration already made a grave mistake by choosing a mediocre man for a complex and difficult job. The lives of the American soldiers and the fate of the Iraqi people are in the hands of this clumsy man, whose self interest prevents the administration from seeing the real problems and causes. This guarantees that only more mistakes will be made. The American soldiers and the Iraqi people will continue to pay for these mistakes with their lives.

*

When writing the above article, I hoped the whole world *except* the Iraqis would read it. To make it sound more reasonable, I left out some very important factors in the insurgent revolt, thinking they might be lost in a rude reality. But I felt that missing part would insult the Iraqi readers.

As Commander-in-Chief, you should notice it too.

The insurgents do not fight only for their jobs and their livelihood. Most people are willing to die for a much more noble cause: protecting their country, their people, and their honors from occupiers.

And these Iraqis, like Americans and people all around the world throughout the history of mankind, have had these same moral values and sense of sacred duty since their elementary school years, these same instincts for survival since birth.

2

READ NEWSPAPERS

If the fate dictates that the President should actively engage as Commander-in-Chief, here is my first piece of advice: *Read the newspapers every morning.*

Don't wait until you get to the Oval Office and sit solemnly behind your desk to read the carefully limited and rosy press reviews prepared by your staff. You can sip your latte and scan the news covering the war while having breakfast in the kitchen nook with the First Lady. You don't have to read the whole article, just pay close attention to *all details leading to the death of each soldier*. It shouldn't take more than a few minutes.

If President Bush had cared to read the papers in that manner, I am sure that, in the first few months into the war, he would have encountered plenty of news reports that would help him find a way to respond quickly to protect the lives of our soldiers.

A few months after we invaded and occupied Iraq, there were at least seven senseless deaths of U.S. troops:

> -*One was shot in the neck while shopping in a Baghdad flea market.*
> -*One was shot in the head while waiting to buy some water on a university campus.*
> -*Three were killed by a grenade while guarding a children's hospital.*

-One died while on sentry duty at a museum.
-One sacrificed his life when his superiors gave him the important responsibility of watching over a...gas station.

The circumstances under which the first two soldiers were killed — one at a flea market, the other while trying to buy some water – must have given the President an unpleasant insight: Those soldiers were the first victims of the strategists and military experts in his administration.

These experts had envisioned a scenario in which the Iraqis would merrily welcome American soldiers as heroes and liberators with bouquets of flowers. The two young soldiers, trusting the cheerful predictions of their leaders, had nonchalantly walked amid the crowd, thinking that the Iraqi students and citizens milling around loved and admired them. Instead, the enemies shot both of them dead at close range with a bullet in the neck or head in broad daylight.

The five other senseless deaths — *Three when guarding a children's hospital, one on guard at a museum, one while watching over a gas station* — should reveal certain degree of abnormality apparent in the talent, the ethics, the experience and the intelligence of the Secretary of Defense Donald Rumsfeld as well as of Ambassador L. Paul Bremer.

In late July 2003, troops from the Fourth Division, U.S. Army, were given the task of guarding and protecting the children's hospital in Baqubah, northeast of Baghdad. It was a boring assignment and a number of soldiers sought a little fun by playing chess. The enemy passed by, saw the easy target, and tossed a grenade onto the chessboard. Three soldiers died; four others were severely wounded. The news bulletin included an ironic detail: The grenade thrower had chosen to perform his deed at a time when there were not many people around. That means he took care not to harm other Iraqis and the children; his sole aim was to kill Americans. (*It could also mean if that grenade thrower were given the task of protecting his own people and the Iraqi children, he could have done it as well as the American soldiers.*)

By then, Ambassador Bremer already completed his plan to disband the entire Iraqi armed forces, police and security personnel.

If only Bremer had executed his plan as slowly and leisurely as he performed the task of rebuilding Iraq, and hundreds of thousands of Iraqi soldiers, police, security personnel hadn't been totally laid off, he could have chosen a couple of hundred from those people and dispatched them to sentry duty at the hospital, at the museum, or the gas station. But the Iraqi army had been quickly and completely liberated from their wage-earning jobs at that time. With nothing to do then, they might have attended clandestine meetings in their homes or spent free time making bombs to fight the Americans and "re-liberate" their country.

And so five American warriors died senseless deaths while being forced to steal the jobs of Iraqi security guards, soldiers or policemen.

The death of Private First Class Edward J. Herrgott, from Shakopee, Minn., should tell you a lot about the character of two key leaders in Iraq war. You'll see in his death: Secretary Rumsfeld's misjudgment of the serious consequences of the occupation and Ambassador Bremer's headline-grabbing, boastful, unconscionable and irrational actions.

At the time, Bremer had just assumed his post in Iraq. The situation there was reaching a boiling point. The leader of the liberation force had to take up residence and work within the "Green Zone", surrounded by impenetrable walls and fortresses. While moving around, he had to crawl into an armored car so the Iraqis, who had just been liberated by the Americans, wouldn't have a chance to…kill him. But lo and behold, at that precise moment, Bremer had a divine inspiration to open the National Museum and invite the media and the diplomatic corps to come and enjoy the antique show.

Consequently, U.S. soldiers were dispatched to the museum to stand guard and maintain orders and security while the high and mighty savored the sight of the Iraqi antiques. Thus, a number of American troops were placed in a vulnerable position, standing stock-still in front of the museum for hours on end. The snipers, at some distance away, could choose their targets at will.

Apparently, Ambassador Bremer knew that it was perilous to put on such a show. Therefore, the expo was a quickie. Moving at a feverish pace, the event lasted less than three hours. But it was still too late. That day, Private First Class Herrgott was shot dead while standing in the turret of a tank performing sentry duty at the museum. Twenty years was all he got on this earth.

At that point in time, the antique show didn't serve to benefit the strategies and tactics of restoring peace and re-building Iraq. It wasn't a "must do", a "can't delay", or something that couldn't wait until security was better suited for such an event.

In fact, it served one single purpose: Helping the ambassador earn his stripes with his boss and look good before the media. It gave his boss and the entire U.S. the impression that, in just a few months after Bremer had been at his post in Iraq, peace had been restored in that nation. It showed that marketplaces, schools, hospitals and even museums (considered a luxury) had resumed their normal activities. If the media raved about having a chance to attend the antique show in Baghdad, Bremer's reputation as a genius in restoring peace and conquering the enemies would spread around the world.

That unconscionable, senseless, and dishonest act, however, cost Private Herrgott his life.

Reading the newspapers every morning, you would certainly notice as well a type of fatality that gives you a knot in your stomach: Our soldiers on patrol have been killed when their vehicles ran over the bombs or they were ambushed. These fatalities have occurred not occasionally but quite regularly; a few every day, day after day, month after month, and year after year.

As Commander-in-Chief you should be curious and wanted some questions answered: How essential were those patrols that Americans had to risk their lives? How important were those patrols to the tactics and strategy of the U.S. Armed Forces that their commanders were ready and willing to send, on a daily basis, three or four soldiers into their deaths?

One way to find out is go over the daily assignment sheets for each patrol squad, or, as I have suggested, just read the newspapers. One AP reporter provided a very interesting item, the assignment sheet of an 8-member squad led by Second Lieutenant Peter Balke.

Chris Tomlinson described this squad's three main objectives on a day in mid-March as follows:

1. *Stop by the Jordanian Embassy to check security*
2. *Count the squatters in an old government building*
3. *Investigate complaints that a new brothel had opened.*

Yes, you read it correctly — the high and mighty sent them out on patrol to check out a *brothel!*

By then, the number of American soldiers killed and wounded while on patrol was already in the thousands. And Second Lieutenant Balke and his 8-man squad still had to risk their lives to invade a...prostitute den, eliminating the headquarters of the pros, who, perhaps suffering from hunger and poverty, were forced to make use of the God-given weapon to terrorize their Johns' wallets.

On that day, Lieutenant Balke's squad was very lucky. Although they didn't accomplish the task – they arrived a bit late and failed to capture the prostitutes — still their patrol cars didn't run over any bombs or fall in an ambush. All eight of them returned to their base in one piece.

As Commander-in-Chief, you should be aware of the activities and the fates of our soldiers on the battlefield by the time you reach your office, the highest of the land. Read it first, and think deeply about it.

Those five or ten minutes of serenity will remind you of the responsibility you possess as supreme leader. You will remember the thousands of soldiers, who, before being sent to war, respectfully greeted you, stood or sat solemnly for hours to listen to your exhortation; most of them with eyes filled with trust.

And you will remember that, by ordering the American soldiers into war to defend their country you are given, in the same instant, a tremendous responsibility by this nation, by their families, their loved ones and by those soldiers themselves. You are to use all your talents and all your strength to protect the military.

The soldiers' duty is to willingly sacrifice their lives to defend their country. Your duty is to pour your heart and mind into the task of protecting them. This nation and her people have given you all the power and resources to do the job.

But in this situation, you can save lives of at least some American soldiers without using all such power and resources. You don't even need the experiences of a professional military man or a general's knowledge of strategies and tactics on the battlefield. The only weapon you need is your common senses.

Just pick up the phone, speak to the Secretary of Defense or the general in charge, telling them about your concerns and making sure that from now on no American soldiers in Iraq should risk their lives for the task of counting the squatters or attacking a newly opened brothel.

3

Read Books

My second advice, "Read books," was originally designed for Commander-in-Chief George W. Bush only. It's too late now, and was already too late when I first gave it. But I say it again because it has never been outdated for history, since in the future history might repeat itself and produce for America another president who doesn't like to read books.

If you don't want to, that's fine, Mr. President, but you should, however, request your staff to read. They don't have to turn themselves into bookworms, but should read whatever will assist them in doing a better job.

At least two statements in your *second inauguration address* could have been avoided had this measure been done earlier. The first is a phrase that is an insult to all Americans of average intelligence. The other is a statement that offends a large part of the world's population, those who have had the misfortune of having lived, or possibly died, under totalitarian regime.

I believe you had no idea how boastful and arrogant that speech sounded. But I'll bet you must have known how your father, former President Bush, felt compelled to hold a press conference to defend you and rectify the supercilious statements you uttered.

Following is an excerpt from a news article of the AP published on January 23, 2005, by Deb Riechmann. I hope that it will help you see that your father was not attacking your speech but rather, trying to tone down its heavy-handed rhetoric and trying to close the deep gap between the words and their meaning.

Riechmann wrote: "President Bush's inaugural address, with its emphasis on spreading democracy and eliminating tyranny throughout the world, was not meant to signal a new direction in U.S. foreign policy or to portray America as arrogant, his father said yesterday.

'People want to read a lot into it—that this means new aggression or newly assertive military forces,' former President Bush told reporters during an informal visit to the White House briefing room. ... 'It doesn't mean instant change in every country. That's not what he intends,'"

Your father tried to save you by telling the whole world: "This President didn't mean what he said!"

British Prime Minister Tony Blair, America's closest ally, usually echoes you right away, albeit in finer, more articulate language. This time, however, he seemed uneasy and hesitated to justify what you said. After saying a few nice words about your speech, as per protocol, he lowered his voice and softened the tone: "[The American Administration] know... that you can't just go round invading every country that you think should be a democracy. What you can, however, do is to say that you are going to encourage people to become more democratic and more open." What the Prime Minister was pointing out was that America couldn't go around attacking every nation that is not in alignment with its policies, especially since we have been stretched thin in a war with just one nation. Rather, it would be wiser from now on, to spread democracy by just giving people some encouraging words.

So, in reality, your father and PM Blair were only helping you by re-clarifying those ostentatious and hyperbolic statements your writers had produced. But their comments did not help explain away the statements that insulted the intelligence of the American people and brought on an unprecedented and widespread scorn to the United States.

The first one: *"The survival of liberty in our land increasingly depends on the success of liberty in other lands."*

When you came across such a bizarre proclamation in the draft of your speech, you should have summoned your speech writer into the office to tell him:

"Your idea is fresh and interesting, but it sounds fuzzy. If I used your idea without any proof or evidence – like some sort of numbers to back it up – people might not believe me. I want you to go and try to find some reference in world history about when the fate of liberty in America was dependent on the success of liberty in other lands. And why it has gotten to the point of life and death that we need to rely desperately on other nations' liberty.

"You are a scholar and a man with a vast knowledge. I'm sure you know that other nations' liberty tends to rise or fall rather erratically. It shouldn't be difficult then to find in the history books evidence of when America's liberty began to deeply depending on other nations'.

"Take the situation after World War Two. When many countries fell into the grip of Communism and lost their freedom, did liberty in America suffer a sudden loss? And how much? When Red China invaded, occupied and swallowed Tibet, did the 'dependent' liberty in America lose some weight? Then in 1975, when twenty million South Vietnamese lost both freedom and happiness in one fell swoop, how big of a chunk was chipped away from America's liberty? When the Soviet Union collapsed and many nations in Eastern Europe regained their freedom, how many liberty points did America gain? And recently, when the Russian people started to feel asphyxiated by Putin's change of heart and attempted to reign in freedom, did America's liberty get strangulated as well? Cuba, right under our nose, has had a calamitous regime for decades; will America's 'dependent' liberty stand a chance of surviving or will it expire along with Cuba's?

"See? If you give me those statistics to prove that America's liberty rises and falls along with other nations' fate, I will have evidence to back up that statement. And when I orate, people will believe me and have confidence in what I tell them."

Mr. President, if your speechwriter thought your demand was easy and left for the library in earnest, then we should send him off with these parting words: "Don't come back for your paycheck until you have found those documents." Of course, we are not likely to ever see him again, for there are no books that tell such foolish and absurd tales.

However, if he saw the light and conceded that he shouldn't have the President of the United States make that ridiculous statement, you should console him and, with tenderness, give him some further guidance:

"I know you understand the American people's psyche very well. You also sincerely want to see my persuasiveness bear fruit and win them over easily. The President of the United States should always act 'in America's interest'. When we sent our troops to Iraq and uprooted Saddam, we did it for America's security. And now we have a chance to turn Iraq into a model democracy for the entire Middle East to try and emulate. This is all for America's long-term security too.

"Now that I'm on a roll, and want to liberate the whole world, you guys thought your job is to find me some kind of magical glue to fasten my aspiration to America's interest so the people will feel good and eagerly make sacrifices. You believe that if I'm just trying to persuade Americans to spend more lives and money for some charitable cause, they wouldn't heed my call. Therefore, you came up with such a gem: 'The survival of liberty in our land increasingly depends on the success of liberty in other lands.' to support my cause, believing that you could incite Americans to go out there enthusiastically and seek liberty for the whole world and, in doing so, keep America's liberty… alive. Sorry, but this strange statement doesn't work on the folks who have common sense.

"I also know that you purloined a phrase from one of my predecessors. President Franklin Roosevelt said something similar: 'We have learned that we cannot live alone, at peace; that our own well-being is dependent upon the well-being of other nations, far away.'

"Roosevelt's statement made sense at that time, for he said it in 1945 during World War II. At first, America ducked responsibility and abstained, letting Germany take over Europe and Japan wreak havoc in Asia. Then, when Japan hit Pearl Harbor, America saw the light — seeing that she had lost her secure nonaligned status — and entered the conflict. The American President's declaration at the time — *that our own well-being is dependent upon the well-being of other nations, far away* — was meaningful and well-said.

"Now, you wrote me a speech and hijacked that phrase. But in the process of modifying it into the context of 'the fish need water to survive', you proclaim that 'America's liberty needs the liberty of other people on this earth to survive'… I think it's meaningless. We'll turn ourselves into a dim-witted and naïve creature by, for no reason, giving the dictators of the world too much power, including the power to strangle liberty in America. What if the likes of Fidel Castro and Kim Jong Il thought we really meant it, they then proceeded to exercise their power by choking their people's throats some more in hope that America's 'dependent' liberty would also take its last breath, a spectacle they would be sure to enjoy tremendously. It would be a tragedy for those people and us.

"If we want to persuade the American people to give their blood, sweat, and tears and money by following me to liberate the whole world, it's easy. All we have to do is to change that phrase into: 'The survival of liberty in our land increasingly depends on the state of health of the *terrorists*.' Who dares contradict such an axiom? If someone expresses doubts, I'll tell them to check and see how much liberty they have lost after 9/11; their right to move freely in airports has been taken away. Are they familiar with the Patriot Act?

"If the terrorists' state of health improved, not only liberty in our own country would be affected, but liberty in all the nations in the world. After one terrorist hid a bomb in his shoes, millions of people, regardless of their nationality, have lost their privilege of wearing their shoes while walking through the security gates at the airports.

"If we were successful in blaming the terrorists in such a righteous fashion, it would be easier for me to invade and occupy any country. All I have to do is to declare that the terrorists are present in such a country, then I'll have just cause to hit that place hard. Trying to pin WMDS on someone and then failing to find the incriminating evidence is too much work. Any country could have some terrorists. If it really has none, all it takes is to invade and occupy it, then terrorists will grow like mushrooms. Believe me, I know this very well."

Now, we go to the second statement: *"Liberty will come to those who love it."*

The earlier statement insults only the intelligence of the American people; this one delivers an uppercut at the jaws of billions of people on this earth.

But here, instead of making your scribe read books, you should shine the light directly into his brain by tell him to read the map. You will unfold the world map and ask him to do some math. You shall tell him to add up all those people who are living under an authoritarian regime, then you shall explain to him that:

"The math you just did should show you that there's a huge number of people already living without liberty. The population of the People's Republic of China contributes more than a billion to that number. Yet, you want me to say, 'Liberty will come to those who love it.' You are basically asking me to slander those poor people by saying that they have no desire for freedom. Making the President of the United States of the twenty-first century declare such a sublimely artless statement is a serious crime.

"Think about it! How can you doubt the desire for freedom of a billion people on Mainland China when thousands of Chinese university students risked their lives fighting for it. But alas! Only tanks and guns arrived to greet them in Tiananmen Square, while precious Lady Liberty never showed up. How many Cubans, how many Vietnamese have been in love with liberty for a long time, but she has refused to bless them with her presence? For many of those who loved her so deeply and tried to do something about it, only chains and manacles and death returned their love.

"Did twenty million South Vietnamese decide among themselves to suddenly stop loving freedom after April 30th, 1975? If not, why did Lady Liberty drop them as if they were hot potatoes? Oh, my dear writer, please pay attention to the history of mankind."

At this point, Mr. Commander-in-Chief, I think you have realized the importance of reading books under those circumstances. It would give the scribes in your speech-writing group fewer chances to write irresponsibly. And it would also help keep the supreme leaders of the United States of America from uttering rash and inane statements.

4

A MODEL DEMOCRACY

The primary goal in attacking Iraq was to "remove" Saddam Hussein from power. It took U.S. Forces only three weeks to complete this mission. The neo-con's leaders then proffered Mr. Bush a brand-new strategy: *U.S. Armed Forces must occupy Iraq and then turn it into a model democracy from which to "democratize" the entire Middle East.* I heard that the authors of this strategy were Messrs. Paul Wolfowitz and Douglas Feith.

Asking the American people to spend their wealth and risk their lives to build democracy in Iraq seemed like a reasonable idea and a noble cause. But how would it be possible that the *"Made in America"* democracy of Iraq would then become a model for all her imperial and dictatorial neighbors that would suddenly have the power to eliminate all the bad regimes in the area?

The strategist Wolfowitz gave this explanation: A democratic Iraq will bring prosperity and happiness to its citizenry. Seeing such a spectacular success, her neighbors will drool over her fortune and immediately follow her footsteps and turn themselves into democratic nations. Then imperialism and dictatorship in the Middle East will exist no more!

As far as I know, humanity's history has never witnessed a leader with such a childish and laughable vision.

Mr. Commander-in-Chief,

If you had studiously read books and equipped yourself with basic knowledge of history and humanity, plus a little common sense, you would have responded to such a strategy from your consultants:

"Your scheme is very attractive and I would love to insert it into my speeches to Congress and the U.N. But I do have a tiny problem with it and hope you will enlighten me.

"Right now in the world, there are plenty of models for democracy. If someone doesn't care for British democracy or French or Canadian or Australian democracy, etc... A very good model for democracy exists right here in the United States of America. It has been around for over two hundred years and has been a colossal presence, stretching from the Atlantic to the Pacific. Why haven't countries in the Middle East adopted such an established model of democracy? Why do they make it harder for themselves by waiting for the U.S. to tear Iraq apart and force-feed it democracy before going democratic themselves? Are these Middle Eastern people Extra-Terrestrials or something? How can they be so stupid, naïve, and shortsighted?

"Was this because the Middle East is so far from America? If they don't see us, they cannot imitate us? But if that's the case, how come Cuba has not been infected? They are right at our doorstop.

"Is it because the Cubans look so different from Americans while the people in the Middle East look like our twins? Then what about North and South Vietnam? They are the same people. They even belonged to the same country. Why didn't the North democratize after the model in the South? Why did the North invade and occupy the South? Why did the North force the South Vietnamese to follow its model of un-democracy under an authoritarian regime controlled by the Communist Party?"

"We can also see clearly that Taiwan is a shining example of a model democracy for the rest of the region. The People's Republic of China is only a few miles away but has refused to follow Taiwan's model. Instead, it has been trying to transform Taiwan into one of its provinces and force

the Taiwanese to live under the Communist Made-in-China model. How odd!

"Also, how can you strategists miss the example of South Korea, a wealthy, developed, democratic nation? North Korea is poor, under-developed, its people have suffered greatly for several decades under a dictatorship. Why is it that North Korea has not followed the model of democracy just south of its border?

"Let's consider the fairy tale in which this strategy is potentially successful, or, in other words, let's assume that the Middle East will follow the example of a model democracy as you believe. I have a suggestion: Select Kuwait as the model nation. The Kuwaitis are indebted to America because we liberated them. And if this country resists democracy, we can easily bring it to them by force. It would be no big deal! This is a tiny and weak nation, which even Saddam Hussein invaded and occupied, so it can't be a challenge for a super-power like America. With Kuwait becoming a model democracy, the whole Middle East, including Iraq, will happily democratize, thus proving your strategy to be a sound one. This is called winning the war in Iraq without having to go there and fight it. What do you guys think?"

Well, war is no joke. So we should start a serious talk. There are two fatal mistakes in Messrs. Wolfowitz and Feith's strategy:

1.   The authors *underestimated* the intelligence, knowledge, and level of education and civilization of the people living in the Middle East.

2.   The author *overestimated* the right to choose the regime and the power to sway the fate of a nation of the people living under a dictatorship.

Mr. Wolfowitz must have looked way, way down on the level of education and civilization of the entire population of the Middle East. He must have thought they were barbarians who were still living in the Stone Age or in the jungles and never, ever had any contact with the civilized world. That was why he decided that they did not give a hoot about democracy, had no idea how beneficial democracy has been

28

to America, Britain, France... And his solution for their salvation was for him to come to their rescue by talking the American President into shoving a model democracy under their noses, and thus making them open their eyes, learn, and "democratize" themselves.

Mr. Wolfowitz reasoned that, seeing a democratic Iraq with its prosperity and happiness, the people in the Middle East would aspire to the same. That is the second fatal mistake.

That kind of argument proves that Mr. Wolfowitz had not a scintilla of understanding about the lives of the people under a totalitarian regime. He thought they could go on a shopping spree, picking up a model democracy and taking it home to apply on the whole nation. He also thought they could order their leaders around and make a regime change. Mr. Wolfowitz thought all those people had to do was to look into their neighbor's backyard and search for a model democracy; once they found it, they would tell their leaders to imitate the model and transform their government into its carbon copy.

(If Mr. Wolfowitz would think a tiny bit more deeply, he would have discovered this: If the people in the Middle East could choose a regime with such ease, they would have been the "Boss" of their nation and their nation would have been no less than really democratic. Why would they need a liberator then?)

The people in the Middle East, as well as most of those living under a dictatorship, are not as dumb as Mr. Wolfowitz thinks. The kings and emperors, despots and presidents in those countries who have used an iron fist on their subjects are not so dumb either. Everyone knows about freedom and democracy. But a brutal emperor fears the loss of his throne. His subjects, though they yearn for freedom and democracy, fear for their lives. Not only can they not choose a regime, they often lose the right to live like human beings. Even when they do not resist, but only complain about the dictatorship and the rule of the Party — as the Chinese, North Koreans, Cubans, and Vietnamese and others know too well – that would be enough for their houses to be invaded by a truckload of police. That's why all the greatest liberators in history have followed a strategy: Get rid of the dictator first!

If Messrs. Wolfowitz and Feith had spent time reading history books, they would have found out that Eastern Europe turned democratic only when the Red Boss — the Soviet Union — was taken off their backs. Freed from the chains and manacles, they scrambled to find democracy. They did not wait for the United States of America to send Paul Bremer over to teach them how.

Well, we don't even have to turn back to the past to learn from it. Just look at the current events unfolding in front of our eyes. While the American President declares a new strategy in spreading democracy by setting up a *model*, the U.S. armed forces have sought democracy for Iraq with an ancient strategy: Dethrone Saddam Hussein first.

Since all the dictators in Middle East are still in power, and most of whom have been allies of America whose interest requires the protection of their thrones, we should stop insulting the people of the Middle East by implying that they have been living under the regime of their choice.

5

THE TWO STRATEGISTS

How brilliant are Messrs. Paul Wolfowitz and Douglas Feith in fact? How could they author such an unenlightened strategy?

With regards to formal education, that's a given. Both men graduated from prestigious universities; Wolfowitz even holds a doctorate in Political Science. Naturally, an individual must possess a great deal of talent and intelligence to hold the position of Deputy Secretary of Defense.

But are these two gentlemen really that brilliant?

An article written by Chris Suellentrop in mid-May 2004, in which the author raves about Douglas Feith, provides a clear answer. At the end of the article, Suellentrop said that in the book *Plan of Attack,* reporter Bob Woodward quoted a comment made by General Tommy Franks about Feith. General Franks proclaimed that Mr. Feith is *"the fucking stupidest guy on the face of the earth."*

The co-author of the *"model"* strategy in Iraq is an … stupid guy?

General Franks's observation did not surprise me, but it only satisfied half my curiosity. How about the other co-author?

Without the general's guidance, I had to resort to reading the newspapers to find out. And I found at least one yardstick to measure the intelligent of Paul Wolfowitz.

As I mentioned before, Paul Bremer, who was sent to Iraq to execute the "Model Democracy" strategy, abolished the Iraq army, dismissed the police and civil servants- an act that immediately caused millions of people to loose their right to make a living. And about six million Sunni felt that they had been prejudiced against and pushed to the perimeter of society, becoming the second-class citizens. They, of course, resisted. Not wanting to accept the blame for the situation, Bremer, along with Don Rumsfeld, insisted that terrorists from the neighboring countries were responsible for the resistance.

Those citizens of neighboring countries were volunteering to come to Iraq and fight was a reality, but they were small in number. They came for a host of reasons: they wanted to help Iraq expel the invaders; they hated America; they feared America would use the pretext of seeking democracy to steal Iraq's oil; they didn't like to see their Islamic friends being bullied by America, etc... Whether those reasons were valid or not is another story. But they did clearly state their goals, and did so repeatedly.

Strategist Paul Wolfowitz came up with a new and bizarre reason for the terrorists' insurgency. He said they attacked Americans and American allies because they were afraid of *his* strategy...They feared that it would succeed and turn Iraq into a model democracy, which would spread out and drive the terrorists into the ground.

In February 9, 2003 article in the *Wall Street Journal* entitled "Support Our Troops," he wrote about the terrorists as follows:

"...We do know this: Despite their differences, the criminal remnants of Saddam Hussein's sadistic regime share a common goal with foreign terrorists — to bring back the failure of Iraqi reconstruction and take the country back to the sort of tyrannical prison from which it has just been freed."

The argument that local terrorists and Saddam's remnants would want to bring the country back to the old regime is understandable. But what about the resistance coming from Jordan, Egypt, Saudi Arabia, and Syria? What is in it for them? What would they wish to achieve? To force the people of Iraq live under a dictatorship till the end of time?

This is Wolfowitz's explanation:

"Terrorists recognize that Iraq is on a course towards self-government that is irreversible and, once achieved, will be an example to all the Muslim world who desire freedom, pointing a way out of the hopelessness that the extremists feed on."

Those resonant yet ethereal words were full of shortcomings and ambiguity where shortcomings and ambiguity are not acceptable.

Who are those foreign terrorists in Iraq? What kind of people are they? Why do they fear democracy and freedom to the point that they are willing to cross the border into Iraq and wear the bomb that will tear their bodies into pieces? For what? To stop the democratization of... another country? What state of despair and hopelessness is forced upon the terrorists?

In the history of mankind, only dictators and their toadies were afraid of the spread of democracy. It would case them to lose their precious thrones, their power, and many times even their own lives. If the "model democracy" strategy authored by Wolfowitz were truly as fantastic as promised, it should have scared the soul out of the Presidents of Egypt and Syria, or the Kings of Jordan and Saudi Arabia, and turned them into terrorists themselves. If they chose not to commit suicide bombing, they would have sent troops to fight against the model democracy to destroy it and eliminate the threat to themselves. But no, nobody did that. On the contrary, the Presidents of Egypt, the Kings of Jordan and Saudi Arabia have been trying to eradicate terrorism and keep terrorists from crossing into Iraq.

If the dictators created and supported terrorists, it was not because they wanted to stop Iraq's being democratized, but just to attack the invaders. Most of the terrorists here are not servants or foot soldiers of emperors. They are ordinary citizens, exactly the type of people the strategy "model democracy" is aimed at. They are exactly the part of the population in the Middle East who, according to Wolfowitz, is anxious for model democracy to be born and who would rally around it.

If they had been, as Wolfowitz said, yearning for freedom and democracy as recently as just a few months ago, why the change of heart now? Why did they become fearful of freedom and democracy all of a sudden? And not only do they fear freedom and democracy in the ordinary sense. According to Wolfowitz, they are literally scared to death. They are willing to let their bodies be shredded and torn to pieces in order to stop... democracy.

Remember: In September 2003, Iraq had no democracy. It was under the Americans' control. It was being coerced to become a *"model of a nation being colonized by an imperialist force."* It was "promised" a democracy by the Americans — just a promise. There had not been a sample of democracy in the showroom for visitors to do a little tasting. And yet, Wolfowitz's terrorists were already scared witless.

The American strategist seriously wanted us to believe that his idea had made the terrorists scared out of their minds!

So Wolfowitz thinks that the whole population of the Middle East remains ignorant and illiterate and in the dark about democracy and freedom. And anyone who had inkling about those things wouldn't be allowed to imitate established models but would have to wait until the Americans invaded, occupied and provided them with America's own democratic model.

And Wolfowitz's terrorists are even weirder than that. They were not afraid of the current models of democracy that have inspired and set a shining example for humankind. They were only scared when Wolfowitz advised the U.S. President to *promise* a democracy to Iraq, even though it was still a shapeless, undefined democracy. And in that state of fear, they feverishly tramped on one another to cross into Iraq, detonated body bombs, killing themselves to destroy the model democracy that is taking its own sweet time to materialize!

Wolfowitz didn't stop there.

In the beginning he declared that his doctrine would bring freedom and democracy to the whole Middle East that is, to a couple of hundred million people. Now, in this newspaper article, he declared what he anticipated would be his crowning achievement. He bragged that his doctrine would bring freedom and democracy to... the entire Islamic world - about a billion souls!

Reading all Wolfowitz's assertion, I find myself disappointed with General Franks.

Wolfowitz should not be ranked below Feith. At the very least, the general should award him the title of *"the fucking stupidest strategist on the face of the earth."*

6

THE MAGIC POTION THAT WILL ELIMINATE TERRORISM

President Bush claimed that he liberated Iraq to give the people of the Middle East a model democracy which would lead to democratization of the entire region. But he didn't stop there. This was only a small part of a broader strategy to spread freedom and democracy to all corners of the world. And he said that would lead to his ultimate goal: the elimination of terrorism everywhere. He believes that terrorism will not survive in a world that's ruled by democratic regimes.

In short, in the war on terror, Commander-in-Chief George Bush believes he has found a magic potion: democracy. Drink it and the world will forever be immune to the terrorist virus.

Where did he get this theory?

In Feb. 2005, the American public was given the good new that their President had given up his bad habit of not reading books. The White House informed the *Wall Street Journal* of two of the President's favorite books: Tom Wolfe's *I am Charlotte Simmons* and Natan Sharansky's *The Case for Democracy*. At the same time, Amity Shlaes of *Financial Times* wrote in her column, "President George W. Bush has said that his plan to democratize the Middle East was inspired by Natan Sharansky, the former Soviet dissident and now Israeli politician. Indeed, Mr. Bush has made Mr. Sharansky's recent book, *The Case for Democracy*, his own Middle East Bible."

Sharansky is a famous anti-communist fighter, who spent nine years in the Soviet Union's gulag. After being rescued from Russian's prison system, he became a major political figure in Israel, once serving as a Deputy Prime Minister of his country. With Ron Dermer, he co-authored "*The Case for Democracy: The Power of Freedom to Overcome Tyranny and Terror*." It was a beautiful panegyric about the benefits and powers that freedom and democracy can bring to humanity.

Inspired by the book, Mr. Bush and his advisers came up with a strategy to reach an ambitious goal: destroying terrorism by bringing democracy to the oppressed people of the world.

Sharansky's logic was sound and convincing. In a democratic nation, the law protects its citizens and forbids rulers from abusing their power or oppressing their people. Citizens have rights and many ways of protesting or expressing anger with the government without resorting to violence. Voting is the best tool ever invented by mankind to change a country's leaders. People who live with freedom in a democratic society are much happier than those who live in non-democratic societies and most conflicts between individuals groups can be resolved peacefully guided by the laws of the land. Terrorist tactics are not only unnecessary but condemned. That means people who choose those tactics become losers.

Democracy also compels a nation to live peacefully with its neighbors. Only in a totalitarian regime can the dictator start a war whenever he wants to. In a democratic society the leader needs congressional or parliamentary approval, which means the approval of at least the majority of a population's representatives. And normally, people opt not to go to war.

In short, according to Sharansky and Bush's theory, democracy creates no terrorists, and people who live in a democracy are disinclined to inflict terrorism on their or other nations.

The theory sounds reasonable and strongly convincing. But the reality oftentimes proves the opposite. It was not too hard for the President of a very democratic America to start a war, invading Afghanistan and Iraq, if he had a cause. After 9/11, Americans were terrified and their President could send his military forces anywhere to fight terrorists with big support from Congress. By the same token, the name of democracy didn't stop the U.K. and Italy from joining the U.S. in war even though they weren't Bin Laden's direct victims.

Indeed freedom and democracy create the societies with a low level of conflicts, hatred, and resentment, but the belief that they can eradicate those problems for mankind is dangerously naïve.

Mark Helprin, the author of *The Pacific and Other Stories*, wrote in *The Wall Street Journal*: "…no law of nature says a democracy is incapable of supporting terrorism, so even if every Islamic capital were to become a kind of Westminster with curlicues, the objective of suppressing terrorism might still find it death in the inadequacy of the premise. Even if all the Islamic states became democracies, the kind of democracies they might become might not be the kind of democracies wrongly presumed to be incapable of supporting terrorism." ("Our Blindness" WSJ Jan. 24, 2005)

In the same article, Helprin pointed out the flaw and lack of insight of the democratizing power of a Paul Wolfowitz's Democracy Model:

"And if Iraq were to become the kind of democracy that is the kind wrongly presumed (and for more than a short period), there is no evidence whatsoever that another Arab or Islamic state, without the benefits of occupying armies, would follow. And if they did, how long might it last? They do not need Iraq as an example, they have Britain and Denmark, and their problem is not that they require a demonstration, but rather their culture, history, and secret police."

On Mar. 05, 2005, Harvey Morris, the bureau chief of *The Financial Times* in Jerusalem, added more wise arguments on the same matter:

"One has to look no further than the election in Iraq. The satisfaction felt by the US administration when millions of Iraqis turned up at polling stations in defiance of insurgent threats was tempered by results that showed a majority had shunned Washington's preferred candidates in favour of a clergy-backed Shia slate.

"The trouble with democracy is that, given a free choice, electorates will often make the 'wrong' one, opting for whichever option best challenges the status quo. In many parts of the Middle East, that means the Islamists.

"Similar shocks might be in store if and when democracy advances elsewhere in the region. Should the Islamic Hamas party contest Palestinian parliamentary election in July, it will almost certainly dent the secular Fatah movement's dominance.

"...In Lebanon, where street demonstration have forced the resignation of a pro-Damascus cabinet, there is no guarantee that an eventual withdrawal of the Syrian army will not strengthen the legitimacy of Hizbollah, which Washington also regards as a terrorist organization."

Less than one year later, political events in Middle East unfolded with the negative results of the democratic process almost exactly as the predictions of these two writers. Actually, the reality was more depressing than their warnings.

The democracy that Bush administration hastily forced on Palestine's President created a Hamas government which not only supported terrorists but itself had been named by the U.S. and the West a terrorist organization. And the Bush staff immediately started seeking help from allies to boycott, isolate, and even try to destroy it. (Our ally Israel has to help Mr. Bush with damage control by jailing a large number of newly elected Hamas legislators. And in Jan. 2009, while Israeli forces attacking Hamas in Gaza, Israeli Vice Premier Haim Ramon flatly said, "What I think we need to do is to reach a situation in which we do not allow Hamas to govern.")

Apparently, all the evidence of such a sad reality never reached Commander-in-Chief Bush. As of today, Mr. Bush still believes in the magic effect of Sharansky's potion.

If we trust President Bush's judgment and intelligence, and are willing to give his strategy another chance to show its capability of destroying terrorism, we still have no hope. For even if democracy and freedom can really deny the terrorists a place to be born and grow, they have no power to prevent the existence of a terrorist like Osama bin Laden.

Tyrants and dictators indirectly produce insurgents and terrorists-Sharansky was absolutely right about that. But we have to be very careful here. The oppressed citizens, who revolted, fought back totalitarian regimes, or even overthrew evil kings, were oftentimes not called terrorists but freedom fighters, liberators, democratic activists, human rights heroes, etc… Natan Sharansky was once among them, though he never used violent means to gain back his freedom from the Soviet tyrants.

Whether they apply peaceful or violent tactics, are the "good guys" or "bad guys", these rebellious forces have one thing in common: They attack their dictators, their own tyrants. They fight back against their own rulers. They don't cross borders and go into another country to kill its citizens in order to show the hatred and the anger they harbor against their own ruthless government.

If Osama Bin Laden were the product of a totalitarian government, meaning he was a victim of the Saudi King's oppression, and if he yearned for democracy and freedom, then he should have attacked the Saudi royal family, as common sense and history would dictate. What kind of logic compelled him to dedicate his heart and mind to attacking and killing Americans in New York?

Bin Laden was never a victim of Saudi Arabia's regime in the way an ordinary citizen might be. Belonging to a very wealthy family, and being highly educated, he could have enjoyed all the privileges reserved for the elite. He has nothing against the Saudi royal family's dictatorship, and apparently, he has no concern about human rights or woman's rights in his country. He condemns the Saudi government only because the Kingdom is a close ally of America, and because it allowed the U.S. soldiers to be stationed on Saudi soil.

His reason for attacking America –as he said from the beginning and repeated many times later- was the American bases in Saudi Arabia, a fact that he deemed sacrilegious. Fifteen out of the nineteen terrorists on 9/11 were his countrymen. When America struck back, he added more "noble causes" such as "fighting for Palestine," "fighting again the Crusaders who started a religious war against Muslim believers," etc.

If President Bush were talented and lucky enough to bring democracy and freedom to the whole world, the kind of terrorist like bin Laden would never go away.
Occasionally this type of terrorist emerges out of thin air. They attack us, not because America or their own country doesn't have enough democracy or perfect freedom. They want to destroy us just because the American government failed to act as they wanted.
So even if Sharansky's magic potion should happen to reach Saudi Arabia, eliminating the Kings' regime and turning that nation into a model democracy, bin Laden's thinking wouldn't change. Democracy in his country wouldn't make him hate America less.

That's why America, after hundreds of years as a model democracy, still suffers from the terrorist acts of people like Tim McVeigh, Eric Rudolph, Edgar Ray Killen.

McVeigh bombed a federal building in Oklahoma City, killing nearly 200 people to show his anger toward the government's actions at Waco. Rudolph hated gays and abortions and also resorted to killing. Killen discriminated against blacks, killed three young men who were activists for the cause of black people's rights and equality… Whether hating American government, as Tim Mcveigh and bin Laden did, or harboring an enmity to special groups of Americans, as Rudolph and Killen did, these kinds of terrorists are immune to Sharansky's magic pills. Here, the nature of the nation's government has nothing to do with the formation of the mind of the terrorists.

And here's the big problem: If Sharansky's medicine were as effective as he says, it would only serve as a vaccine, its capacity, at best, to destroy the environment in which terrorist bacteria can be born and grown. It prevents terrorism in the future, but it does not cure the existing sickness from which America is now suffering.

Religiously believing in this magic formula, Mr. Bush has spent billions of dollars and thousands of American lives to buy himself a future world free of terrorism. He has been leading the country in a chase after a vaccine that may perhaps be effective in the unforeseeable future. And bin Laden, the terrorist America wanted to eliminate the most, is still alive somewhere in the mountains of Pakistan, totally outside the range of Sharansky's magic potion.

7

NATAN SHARANSKY

Natan Sharansky was once my hero. He had a dream that I, and perhaps the majority of the globe's population, wanted to share: *freedom and democracy for the whole world*. He was determined to realize it and executed his plan with a great deal of wisdom.

Since America is the only superpower rich and strong enough to make his dream come true, he approached the American President and convinced him to take on the task.

Starting a war to bring democracy to another country is a noble cause. But that cause is not strong enough for President Bush to move his country toward spending American resources and blood. Sharansky immediately provided an offer the Americans couldn't refuse: A world full of democratic governments will eliminate terrorists; by realizing Sharansky's dream, President Bush would bring safety to America and peace to the world.

With America's security at stake and two wars already started, the only thing Mr. Bush had to do is stay the course and bring freedom and democracy to Iraq. This newly liberated country would, according to Sharansky's theory, get rid of all tyrants and dictators in Middle East, at least.

President Bush religiously believes in Sharansky's theory. Not long after their first meeting in the White House, Sharansky wrote a book which his new convert considered a Bible for the Middle East strategy.

Like Mark Helprin, I could find no logic or "natural law" that supports Sharansky's theory. I believed that Sharansky knew that too, and he fed it to Mr. Bush anyway because the president of the U.S. badly needed a huge benefit to promise Americans, to justify his action and any war he created.

Sharansky's strategy for fighting terrorists didn't make sense. But his tactics to lure Mr. Bush into spending Americans' lives and treasure to spread democracy throughout the globe were almost perfect. I admired his intelligence and his ethics until April 24, 2006, when his article *"Dissident President"* appeared in The *Wall Street Journal.* In that article he tried to explain some of the president's big failures, to comfort and encourage Mr. Bush, and praise his tenacity for "staying the course."

Sharansky wrote:

"There are two distinct marks of a dissident. First, dissidents are fired of ideas and stay true to them no matter the consequences. Second, they generally believe that betraying those ideas would constitute the greatest of moral failures. Give up, they say to themselves, and evil will triumph. Stand firm, and they can give hope to others and help change the world.

Political leaders make the rarest of dissidents. In a democracy, a leader's lifeline is the electorate's pulse. Failure to be in tune with public sentiment can cripple any administration and undermine any political agenda. Moreover, democratic leaders, for whom compromise is critical to effective governance, hardly ever see any issue in Manichean terms. In their world, nearly everything is colored in shades of gray.

That is why President George W. Bush is such an exception. He is a man fired by a deep belief in the universal appeal of freedom, its transformative-power, and its critical connection to international peace and stability. Even the fiercest critics of this idea would surely admit that Mr. Bush has championed them both before and after his re-election, both when he was riding high in the polls and now that his popularity has plummeted, when criticism has come from longstanding opponents and from erstwhile supporters.

With a dogged determination that any dissident can appreciate, Mr. Bush, faced with overwhelming opposition, stands his ideological ground, motivated in large measure by what appears to be a refusal to countenance moral failure..."

You see here about one fourth of the article in which Sharansky fawns on Mr. Bush, comparing him to a certain type of hero of modern time: the dissidents. According to Sharansky, President Bush possesses all the characteristics of those heroes who risk their freedom, even their lives, fighting against tyrants, dictators, and oppressors. According to Sharansky, our leader belongs to a group of extraordinary human beings who are willing to sacrifice themselves for others' rights, freedom and justice. And he is unique, because no other politicians have these qualities.

And he praises Mr. Bush for standing his ideological ground whether he was riding high in the polls, or when his popularity plummeted, even when faced with overwhelming opposition... Sharansky deceived the President by making him believe that he became unpopular because he refused to abandon his great ideas. As far as I know, no one opposes or criticizes Mr. Bush because of his ideas or his dream of saving the world. People only criticize, and are angry with him because of his actions, tactics, and the strategy he pursued in realizing his dream. His ideas bother nobody; only his incompetence and poor governing skills cost him his popularity.

Sharansky continued: *I myself have not been uncritical of Mr. Bush. Like my teacher, Andrei Sakharov, I agree with the president that promoting democracy is critical for international security.*

He hasn't yet stopped flattering Mr. Bush! I found in the above statement a very sophisticated fawning tactic that intended to make the president feel much prouder and happier than when calling him a modern hero. When Sharansky says that he and his teacher, Andrei Sakharov, **agree** with the president… he distorts the truth (that "the president" actually took the ideas from Sharansky and follow the "Bible" that Sharansky created). The word *"agree"* instantly turns Mr. Bush into the "author," the creator of the strategy of "eliminating terrorists with democracy". Suddenly, he becomes a brilliant leader with a great vision for America and the world. Sharansky and his teacher have modestly stepped aside, taking on the minor role of admirers of the great leader George W. Bush!

Before reaching a point where Mr. Bush might burst with pride, Sharansky then lays down his criticism:

But I believe that too much focus has been placed on holding quick elections, while too little attention has been paid to help build free societies by protecting those freedoms - of conscience, speech, press, religion, etc. - that lie at democracy's core.

I believe that such a mistaken approach is one of the reasons why a terrorist organization such as Hamas could come to power through ostensibly democratic means in a Palestinian society long ruled by fear and intimidation.

This really surprised me.

This kind of argument belongs to someone from another planet ignorant of all mankind's history, especially the major events of the last century. In Eastern Europe, after overthrowing their Communist governments, eliminating tyrants, those nations have found democracy themselves, and never needed to invite Americans to come and *"build free societies by protecting the freedoms of conscience, speech, press, religion, etc."* before holding elections. Not one of those nations fell into a disastrous war as did Iraq. And the mistakes made by the occupation forces in Iraq are not only due to *"too much focus on holding quick elections."* Sharansky knows this well.

The next paragraph, explaining why Hamas won the election in Palestine, is more peculiar. Sharansky thinks the Palestinians voted wrongly because they live in a society *"long ruled by fear and intimidation,"* meaning that if they had not been scared, oppressed, bullied, and abused, they wouldn't have put the Hamas organization in power.

By Sharansky's thinking, this would eliminate from the list of those citizens who vote "correctly" almost everyone who has lived, is living under a dictator or oppressor. To be qualified, they should at first ask the tyrants to rule nicely, without intimidation and fear!

But here is the funniest part: Who has been intimidating the Palestinian and creating terror in their society for so long? Sharansky is not specific, but, of course, the readers should understand that he is pointing to the terrorist organizations like Hamas and Fatah. They are to blame for every bad thing that has happened in Palestine, including causing Palestinians to vote wrongly.

If we agree with Sharansky's logic, we would be terribly unfair to the Palestinians, insulting their intelligence. According to him, Palestinian society has been long ruled by terrorist organizations using fear and intimidation. Now that they have the right to choose freely, the majority immediately voted into power the evil force that terrorized them! Can Palestinians be that stupid?

No people are that stupid. Like all of us, the Palestinians choose the ones who they believe are fighting effectively against their enemies or anyone who is doing them harm. So, to be honest, Sharansky should say: Palestinian society, long ruled by terror of... *Israel,* voted for Hamas, who happen to be on our terrorist list, but are considered heroes by their fellow countrymen.

But of course Sharansky and this Bush-flattering article cannot handle that truth. He has to avoid any statement that might damage his country's reputation and sabotage his agenda. He chooses to make his intentioned reader, President Bush, swallow his absurd logic instead.

After criticizing Mr. Bush's for only the mistake of doing two good things (*holding elections, help build free societies*) in the wrong order, Sharansky started praising him profusely. His agenda clearly shows throughout the article. He ties the President to Sharansky's idea, forces him to loyally follow his "Bible" and stay the course.

"[B]etraying those ideas would constitute the greatest of moral failures. Give up... and evil will triumph." With statements like these, he puts our President in splendid mansion but one with no exits. President Bush cannot back out, unless he is willing to accept his *greatest of moral failures* and to *allow the evil to win.* By doing that, Mr. Bush, besides being morally bankrupt, would also lose his heroic title "The Dissident President," a crown never before awarded to a politician.

With this article, Sharansky holds the President of the U.S. hostage, obligated to work for *his* (Sharansky's) idea in pride for, at least, the rest of his presidential term.

I have nothing against Sharansky's idea. Actually, "spreading freedom and democracy throughout the world" is also my wish, my dream. And witnessing the way Sharansky has tricked President Bush into accepting the responsibility of a world-savior, I see in him a very clever and intelligent man. He is aware of Mr. Bush's limitations and takes advantage of them by feeding him arguments and logic that defy common sense.

He also possesses the skill to communicate effectively with Mr. Bush. The vocabulary he uses in the article is well chosen for persuading a very religious president. He bundled all tyrants, dictators, and terrorists into one word, *"evil",* promoting Sir (Knight) George W. Bush, who fights evil, to the rank of Saint who performs divine assignments. That would strongly convince a president who always seeks divine guidance.

But writing such an article three years after the Iraq invasion without mentioning any serious mistakes by the Bush administration is heartless and cruel.

Sharansky is intelligent enough to know that President Bush and his staff have been incompetent, making poor judgments, and committing grave errors, causing the deaths of thousands of Americans and even more Iraqis. Instead of using his intelligence and wisdom to advise Mr. Bush on how to solve the problems, Sharansky just gives the President more illusions and pushes him deeper into a bloody mess.

Imagine this: The village needs a lot of wells dug. A wise man finds a giant who seems able to do the job. He tricks the giant by telling him that there's gold hidden deep down in the ground. Everybody praises the wise man's good intention, and understands why he has to lie to motivate the giant.

But the giant starts showing that physically and mentally he is not up to the task, and instead of digging wells, he destroys the houses, the gardens, property, hurting himself and the villagers in the process. Then the wise man should intervene. He should use his wisdom to teach the giant how to avoid mistakes and do the right thing, or at least, stop him from going further into the insane destruction.

But the wise Sharansky here mentioned no real mistakes. He just created an illusion in which the giant finds himself a hero who has been on the right track all the times. He doesn't seem to care much about American and Iraqi lives.

That is cruel. I may admire Sharansky for his intelligence, talent and his dream, but I cannot tolerate his selfish and inhuman attitude.

So my Dear Commander-in-Chief,

You should be very careful with anyone who can mimic God's language in suggesting or compelling you to play God. Before taking the bait, you should think really hard about the limitations of our country's power and resources, and of your talent, too.

8

OFFENSIVE DIPLOMACY 101

Our Secretary of State, Dr. Condoleezza Rice, is a bright, intelligent and highly educated woman. Her fans, impressed by her talent, begged her to run for President in 2008. She has humbly declined. That fact adds credit to her personality. I once believed that she would bring a great deal of wisdom to the State Department. That's why I was surprised and horrified when I saw her incompetent diplomatic skills displayed in front of the whole world.

On October 9, 2006, North Korea tested a nuclear bomb in defiance of President Bush's warnings and threats. With enormous pressure from the U.S., the United Nations passed a resolution applying economic sanctions on North Korea. Secretary Rice immediately traveled around the world to persuade other nations to punish Kim Jong Il. From Japan and South Korea, Rice received full cooperation. At Peking, though, she expected a struggle because China is North Korea's sponsor, so she was surprised when they seemed to go along with the idea. China's leader was very accommodating. "I cannot conceive of even a short time ago China agreeing to call North Korea's behavior a threat to international peace and security," she said.

Leaving Peking, Secretary of State Rice headed to the last destination: Moscow. Elated by the successes obtained so far, she took a more aggressive stance, telling the Russian leaders that siding with the U.S. in punishing North Korea, and Iran, as well, is the right thing to do.

North Korea was not much of a problem, since Russia doesn't have a close relationship with it. But Iran is a different story. Russia has provided Iran with nuclear technology, equipment, and scientists to produce the atomic capability that caused all the fuss in the first place. Both countries share many common interests. Actually Russia protects Iran as one of its favorite clients.

The warm relationship between Russia and Iran is a formidable obstacle, the cold one between Russia and America is another. So far, the U.S. President and Vice President have strongly implied that President Vladimir Putin is turning into a dictator. During his last visit to Moscow, during a press conference, Mr. Bush bluntly lectured President Putin concerning democracy, freedom, human rights, etc., resulting in an ironic response from the irritated host. Mr. Putin said he believes the Russian people don't want the kind of democracy Mr. Bush is creating in Iraq. The reporters had a good laugh.

With all the Putin bashing from U.S. leaders, it would be hard for Secretary Rice to ask President Putin a favor like betraying his favorite client, Iran, to please the U.S. Apparently, she knew well the difficulty of her task. She flew to Moscow several hours before the scheduled meeting with Russian leaders at the Kremlin. I thought she would have used this time to make some overtures and exchange pleasantries to win over the Russian leader.

Recognizing what was at stake, I was curious and excited. I paid carefully attention to Secretary Rice's actions on October 21, 2006 during the hours before the meeting between the Secretary of State of the U.S. and the President of Russia. The brilliant diplomacy that turns an enemy into a friend is a phenomenon I don't want to miss. I learned the details of that magic moment from a report by Glenn Kessler of *The Washington Post*, October 22, 2006.

MOSCOW – Secretary of State Condoleezza Rice interrupted her diplomacy on the North Korean nuclear crisis yesterday to meet with the son of a slain

Russian journalist and top editors of her newspaper, warning, "the fate of journalists in Russia is a major concern."

Rice's high-profile meeting, scheduled at the request of the State Department, came shortly before she met with Russian President Vladimir Putin, primarily to discuss Russia's implementation of sanctions on North Korea for testing a nuclear device.

…Anna Politkovskaya, a veteran journalist who had sharply criticized the Kremlin and its proxies in the conflict in Chechnya, was shot four times Oct. 7, presumably for her reporting. No senior Russian officials attended her funeral, which attracted thousands of mourners.

"Anna Politkovskaya was a particularly well-known and well-respected journalist, so I think it's important to note that," Rice told reporters traveling with her as she flew to Moscow from Beijing, previewing the comments she made to the editors of Novaya Gazeta, the newspaper where Politkovskaya had worked.

Novaya Gazeta is "one of the best independent voices in Russia," Rice said, noting there is still an independent print media and some independent radio in Russia. Unfortunately, there is not much left of independent television in Russia.

Ultimately, none of Dr. Rice's words conveyed any attempt to improve America's relationship with President Putin. Instead, she put on the standard guise of this administration with its idealistic rhetoric regarding democracy and freedom and accused another world leader of being a dictator. Her statement might win hearts and minds of the Russian people, but certainly not Mr. Putin's.

Diplomatic language is superficially courteous, gentle, and tactful, especially when it has to mask harsh criticism. But if you translate Secretary Rice's words into everyday language, you would be left with this image: The U.S. Secretary of State sharply slapping Mr. Putin on the face and screaming loudly for the whole world to hear, "Shame on you! You're trying to destroy freedom of speech for the Russian people.

You oppress the media and are setting yourself up to be a tyrant. You were likely involved in the murder of Anna Politkovskaya. The fate of journalists in Russia is a major concern of the American government and myself. I'm warning you!"

My impression of Dr. Rice's press conference as a tirade may seem exaggerated and unfair to her. But it actually is gentle compared with the metaphor used by another American diplomat: **"a poke in the eye."** *"It was not a poke in the eye but the right thing to do,"* One of Rice's aides said, justifying his boss' behavior.

In short, here's Secretary Rice's diplomatic strategy: First, slap President Putin in the face (or, if you prefer, *poke him in the eye*) then smile and ask him to do the U.S. a favor.

President Bush sees in Dr. Rice an excellent Secretary of State. A great number of Americans think she deserves to be President. But based on her diplomatic skills as exhibited in Moscow, I doubt she'd be qualified as a door-to-door salesperson. After entering the house, she would immediately start insulting the homeowner before trying to persuade him to buy her products! Surely her sales record would be very low.

Like most of leaders of our time, President Putin is a bigger- than- life figure, but he is still possessed of the qualities that define most people in terms of his ego and capacity to be offended. He is not a saint who, after being poked in the left eye by Dr. Rice would offer her his right eye. He is not a Buddha, who after being severely abused, can still smile and gently tell her: It's my pleasure to grant your wishes. Please tell me what you want.

So what was the result of the meeting at the Kremlin that day? Secretary Rice didn't say. The State Department also has been mum. After being assaulted by this offensive diplomacy, what did the Russian President say to Dr. Rice? Is he secretly cooperating with the U.S. in punishing North Korea and Iran? How was Secretary Rice greeted at the Kremlin? Was the meeting canceled because the president of Russia was so humiliated — and his eyes were in pain — and he sent Dr. Rice away?

Shortly after that fateful day President Putin announced that he had just delivered $700 million worth of surface-to-air missiles to Iran. The total weapons deal, worth about one billion dollars, had been made with Iran in December of 2005 and included 30 Tor-M1 missile systems' each of which can identify up to 48 targets and fire at two targets simultaneously at a height of up to 20,000 feet (Mike Eckel-AP). The weapons were supposed to be delivered in two years, but Putin expedited the export so that Iran could defend against air strikes from its enemies.

Obviously, all the Putin bashing coming from U.S. officials had an effect. This man became confused and disoriented. And he cooperated with the wrong guys.

An irritated president of Russia is not the only possible victim of Secretary Rice's diplomacy. If Iran and the U.S. get into an armed conflict, some Americans will feel the ultimate effects of her diplomacy as well.

After Secretary Rice dropped her verbal bombs on President Putin, she returned home safely although perhaps downcast. On the other hand, if some day our airmen are ordered by President Bush or any future U.S. President to bomb Iran, they will be greeted with $700 million worth of surface-to-air missiles, courtesy of Mr. Putin.

9

"OUTING" CIA

No, I'm not talking about the case of Valerie Plame.

Like Britain, Italy is a staunch ally of the U.S. and the most loyal one we can find on mainland Europe. Prime Minister Silvio Berlusconi sent 3000 soldiers to Iraq, against the will of 70% of the Italian population, to share the burden of war with the U.S.

On March 4, 2005, U.S. soldiers in Iraq shot to death an Italian intelligence officer: Agent Nicola Calipari, a major general, and the second highest ranking individual in Italy's millitary intelligence agency. He was assigned to Iraq to save Italian citizens who had been kidnapped by the insurgents. In September 2004, he freed two aid workers, Simona Toretta and Simona Pari. In his last mission to save journalist Giuliana Sgrena, he also succeeded. But on the way to the Baghdad airport, heading back to Italy, he, Sgrena, and his driver were fired on. Sgrena and the driver were wounded. Covering Sgrena with his body, Calipari received a bullet to his temple and died instantly.

The soldier who fired the fatal shots told investigators that he and his platoon had set up a checkpoint on the road and saw Calipari's car driving at them too fast, ignoring the soldier's hand and light signals ordering the car to stop. The soldier shot at the engine block to disable it and unfortunately hit all the people inside the car.

"When (Calipari's) coffin returned to Rome," The BBC News reported on 3.6.2005, *"the Italian president and prime minister were there to greet it.*

"President Azeglio Ciampi stood with his hands on the casket in silence for two minutes, later declaring that Calipari would be awarded the gold medal of valour for his heroism.

"... The coffin, wrapped in an Italian flag, was blessed by a military priest and Calipari's own brother, a priest who serves at the Vatican.

"The Pope sent condolences and hailed Calipari a 'hero.'

"...Crowds at football matches across the country observed a minute's silence...

"... The government announced Calipari's body would lie in state ahead of a state funeral."

Obviously, when Calipari lost his life while serving Italy, he had become a hero mourned by his entire nation.

President Bush promised the Italian President that the U.S. would immediately investigate the incident. Italy sent an investigation team to Baghdad to assist American investigators. Later, the findings showed two totally different sets of facts. The Italian investigation found that no clear warning signs were given to Calipari's car, which was traveling at 20 to 30 mph on a road that has no speed limit signs. Italian investigators concluded that stress and inexperience among U.S. soldiers played a major part in the shooting.

The U.S. investigators found that the victims' vehicle was traveling about 50 mph and failed to stop at the checkpoint when ordered to do so. Therefore, they concluded that no disciplinary action should be taken against any soldier involved in the shooting. The killing of agent Calipari and the wounding of his driver and journalist Giuliana Sgrena were judged as justified.

Italy's conclusion faulting the shooters sounded sensitive, sympathetic, and reasonable, almost like the arguments that would be made by the soldier's defense team. The U.S. soldiers committed that crime, Italian investigators argued, because they lacked experience and were put in a stressful situation. This implied that only some light disciplinary actions would be needed like retraining and allowing them time away from duty to recover from the stress of battle.

But for some reason, U.S. military officials in Iraq would not accept any accusation of mistakes made on the part of their soldiers. They would rather the Italian people think that agent Calipari died because his vehicle was speeding and failed to stop when ordered to do so. In short, Calipari had violated the traffic laws that the U.S. Army arbitrarily imposes on Iraq when there is a need for checkpoint.

What kind of traffic law is this? The former Ambassador to Iraq, Paul Bremer, while writing the new traffic laws for the country, did not include the above, and especially not that violation would result in death. Further, U.S. military officials never publicly warned the Iraqis about these new laws.

It seems the only way to learn about them is to study all the incidents in which U.S. soldiers shot at civilian vehicles. (And in addition to "speeding" and "failed to stop when ordered to do so", *"driving too close to a U.S. convoy"* is also a crime that can result in death. An Iraqi Diplomat is trying to find justice for a relative who learned about this law the hard way.)

I carefully read the details of several incidents and have concluded that the current Iraqi traffic laws can be stated as follows:

Driving "too close" to a U.S. convoy is a violation of the U.S. Army's traffic laws and can result in the death penalty- this capital punishment will be applied equally to the driver as well as passengers. How close is "too close" will be judged by any soldier in the convoy who feels a violation is occurring.

The death penalty may also apply to anyone who drives or is a passenger in a "speeding vehicle." The speed limit is not posted and is set based on the opinion of the gunner at the checkpoint.

Failing to stop when signaled by U.S. soldiers to do so because you couldn't see or didn't understand their directions is no excuse, and you will be treated as if you were intentionally defying their orders.

Violators and their passenger(s) receive no tickets, nor will they have the opportunity to defend themselves in court because the penalty is applied immediately. There are no exemptions for minors, and infants in imposing the capital punishment.

The above traffic law can only exist in an occupied country. It is so intolerable that it has to remain secret until it is necessary for the occupiers to justify killing of locals. But since the Italian people are on the side of the occupiers, they found it difficult to accept the fairness of that law.

To add further insult, U.S. millitary officials forbade Italian investigators from making a trip to the crime scene to examine and collect more evidence, asking them instead to sign a report prepared by the U.S. investigation team that confirms that the shooter was clear of any wrongdoing.

The Italian team refused to sign and left in anger.

This situation might be compared to the Rodney King case. On Mar. 03, 1991, King lead Los Angeles police on a high-speed chase and was beaten by officers before being arrested. A bystander videotaped this violent arrest for the whole world to see and his video played on television for months. In the trial that followed, however, the four police officers accused in the beating were acquitted of all charges, sparking the 1992 Los Angeles riots that lasted four days and caused 55 deaths, and 2,383 injuries, and about $1 billion in damage.

The President at the time was George H.W. Bush, a sensitive and wise man, directed a federal prosecutor to bring civil rights charges against the officers in federal court. Two officers were found guilty. Later, King was awarded $3.8 million in a civil case. The matter was closed.

Today, the White House's occupants give no hope to the people of Italy in getting justice for their hero. They have had to find it themselves. *"With U.S. officials choosing to take no disciplinary action against the soldiers, Italian prosecutors almost immediately launched a separate investigation. On Thursday, they narrowed their inquiry to the soldier who fired the fatal shots. He was identified in Italian court document as Spc. Mario Lozano of the Army's New York National Guard."* (Tracy Wilkinson, "Italy may charge U.S. soldier," *Los Angeles Time* 12.23.05)

So the shooter was a National Guardsman newly arrived in Iraq (in just his first few days). This means that the Italian investigators were right in finding him inexperienced and presumably overwhelmed by the stresses of battle. The U.S. military officials' cover-up of his fatal misjudgment is in some ways also understandable. Since there were and are many incidents in which U.S. soldiers shoot at civilian vehicles, occasionally killing entire families, and no one but the victims were found to be at fault, these officials cannot suddenly change their attitude and blame Calipari's death on the gunner. That would show an obvious inconsistency in how the rules are applied.

But Secretary of State Rice cannot act on this logic. She has a duty to protect the relationship between America and Italy, not to justify behind the act of a national Guardsman under duress in urban warfare. She might not care about Agent Calipari and his family, but she should respect the feelings of the people of Italy who just lost a hero. If President Bush was unaware of the seriousness of this situation, Secretary Rice's duty was to inform him of its effect on the citizens of a close ally.

Unfortunately, it seems neither President Bush nor Secretary Rice had any sense of Italy's great anguish. When reporters requested a comment from the State Department about Italy possibly charging Pfc. Mario Lozano, Sean McCormach, its spokesman, said flatly: "This was a tragic situation, but as far as we are concerned, the matter is closed."

With those words, the State Department took their cue from the Defense Department and slapped the people of Italy in the face. The bizarre diplomatic skills of Secretary Rice instantly turned the mistake of one soldier into a horrendous act of arrogant disregard by the U.S. administration.

To defend its honor, Italy slapped back.

The Italian Prime Minister immediately announced that he would withdraw Italian troops from Iraq. In February 2007, an Italian judge indicted Lozano on homicide charges for the fatal shooting of Calipari. Rome prosecutor Franco Ionta told CNN that the trial date was set for April 17, the soldier would be tried in absentia, and no request was made to have him extradited.

That means the trial would be symbolic. By prosecuting this one U.S. soldier, Italian courts have declared that Italy has had enough of U.S. arrogance and deceit. But even worse, this trial would also say to the world that the U.S. military has been systematically covering up their soldiers' crimes, and that there are many Iraqi victims who will never get justice since even a high- ranking officer of an allied Army can't get any.

By this time, however, the significance will be lost since the incompetence and thoughtlessness of this administration have already become obvious to anyone paying attention.

The knock down punch was the Italian judge's issuing of 22 warrants for the arrest of 22 CIA officers. (The list was later updated to 25 CIA operatives and an Air Force Lieutenant Colonel.) Italian prosecutors said that these U.S. officers were involved in the kidnapping of Osama Moustafa Hassan Nasr – also known as Abu Omar – an Egyptian cleric and terrorist suspect, from a Milan street on 2.17.2003. Abu Omar was flown to Germany and then to Egypt where he said he had been held in a Cairo prison and tortured. An Italian prosecutor charged CIA agents with violating Italian law and sovereignty.

There would be no symbolic indictment and justice this time. The warrants allowed for the arrest of the suspects in any of the 25

European Union member countries. They were also sent to the U.S. with a demand for their extradition.

The "suspects" were apparently warned ahead of time because they had safely moved back to U.S. by the time the warrants were issued. But from now on, if any one of them sets foot in Europe, he could be arrested.

Considering all the details of the case, we can't help wondering why Italy would suddenly act against the most important U.S. intelligence agency working abroad. Because when they grabbed Abu Omar, the CIA had the assistance of at least 9 Italian military agents including the spy chief Nicolo Pollari and his deputy, Marco Mancini, head of the counter-espionage office. The operation, which occurred in February 2003, seems not to have violated any laws back then and was kept secret for over a year and a half. But with the death of Agent Calipari and the U.S. mishandling of everything about it, the Italian courts decided this was the right time to make some members of the U.S. Military and CIA pay for what must have seemed to be a profound sense of betrayal.

The Italians have paralyzed CIA operations in Italy at that time. Some of our best spies can no longer work in Europe because their names are on a wanted list. The Italian intelligence agency no longer cooperates with the CIA because one of their top agents was killed by a U.S. soldier and another is about to go to prison for his participation in what they now consider an illegal CIA operation. In January 2007, an Italian magistrate ordered the seizure of a villa owned by former Milan CIA station chief Robert Seldon Lady, a key suspect in the case.

And it didn't stop there. In January 2007, a German court issued arrest warrants for 13 CIA agents for the wrongful kidnapping and imprisonment of Khaled el-Masri, a German citizen of Lebanese descent. Then Spain and Switzerland began targeting CIA agents, too.

These European actions against the U.S. and its agents will make the CIA even more ineffective overseas. Intelligence is one of the most important tools in the war on terror, but soon, in Europe the U.S. will be losing its eyes and ears. Compared to the damage that a furious Italy has done to our CIA operations, the outing of Valerie Plame is a joke.

On top of all this, the Italians withdrew all their troops from Iraq at the end of 2006.

When former President George H.W. Bush found justice for Rodney King it came a little too late. America had lost 55 lives and one billion dollars in the riots. I fear that when his son and Secretary Rice failed to obtain justice for Calipari, the price will be of a much greater magnitude. We won't know its entire cost for years or even decades. But we have already started to make the monthly payments. The vacuum that the 3000 Italian soldiers left in Iraq is being filled with the men and women in the U.S. military.

Before, I had thought only the Defense Department could squander the lives of our soldiers. I was so wrong.

So how can you, the Commander- in- Chief, escape such diplomatic disaster?

Very simple: Do not hire any person who speaks faster than he or she thinks or just speaks without thinking at all. And since the Secretary of State is selling our foreign policy, she or he should possess the common sense of to know what to say, and when and where.

10

DO NOT SHOW YOUR IGNORANCE

At times, you or your cabinet members have to refer to the Vietnam War to explain your foreign policy. It might be helpful if, before you speak, you read the following article written by an expatriate from the Republic of Viet Nam.

Is Ignorance Contagious?

by HOANG DUOC THAO

(This article was written a few days after Secretary of Defense Donald Rumsfeld went on the talk show "Hardball" and insulted the people of the former Republic of Vietnam. Originally, I had put it aside because I felt sorry for this man who had to deal with the headache of the Iraq occupation. But seeing the disaster that has brought to the American soldiers and Iraqis, by the ignorance of the American leadership, I would be guilty of complicity in this tragedy if I kept my silence simply to save Secretary Rumsfeld from a little embarrassment. And now Rumsfeld's ignorance has spread to the "Leader of the Free World." On September 27, 2004, President Bush went on "The O'Reilly Factor" where he confidentially affirmed, "The South Vietnamese did not fight for their freedom." Both the President and the Secretary of Defense owe an apology to the citizens of the Republic of Vietnam, who fought the Communists to the death to protect freedom and

democracy, and the American veterans, who were there sacrificing their lives to help them.)

On April 29th, Defense Secretary Rumsfeld appeared on the talk show "Hardball" with Chris Matthews. Comparing Iraq to Vietnam, he observed that the Communist regime in North Vietnam was "very nationalistic" and the South Vietnamese administration at the time was a "puppet" government that had no constitution and no elections. The exact script ran as follows:

RUMSFELD: Well, in Vietnam, you had a very nationalistic element in North Vietnam—and the Viet Cong that was part of the situation there. And you had a government that was not a popular government in the South. They didn't have—hadn't fashioned their own constitution They hadn't had their own elections They were governments that were considered by the rest of the Vietnamese people to be puppet governments.

MATTHEWS: So the Baathist elements that remain, the remnants, are nowhere as strong, as you believe, in their passion as the V C were and the North Vietnamese were?

RUMSFELD: That's right.

Secretary Rumsfeld's remarks, which demonstrate his poor knowledge of the Vietnam War, appall and frighten me. The Vietnam War era is not so far back in the past as to be irrelevant or forgotten. More importantly, the Vietnam War experience and the lessons learned from it are a crucial and vital part of the United States' war history, which should not be ignored by any Secretary of Defense, especially one who has taken the nation so deeply into war as Secretary Rumsfeld.

I would like to set the record straight on a few key points. There was a very Communist, not nationalistic, element in North Vietnam since 1954. In 1954, after defeating the French, the Communist government quickly sent those Vietnamese Nationalists who still in the North, to their graves or to prison. The Vietnamese Communist regime, whose ultimate goal was to bring the whole world under the red banner of their big comrade, the Soviet Union, never tolerated the Nationalist ideology although they exploited it for their own ends. Even some Nationalist groups who had fought the French alongside the Viet Cong had to share in this bleak fate of death or imprisonment.

One million Vietnamese Nationalists and their families in the North moved South that same year. With the help of the United States, which at the time was vigorously working to stop Communism, Prime Minister Ngo Dinh Diem organized their evacuation and resettlement to the South.

Under the leadership of Prime Minister Diem, who later was elected the first President, South Vietnam became the Republic of Vietnam enjoying the beauty and benefits of the best democratic society that a third world country could offer during wartime. Apparently unbeknownst to Secretary Rumsfeld, we did have a Constitution and did have elections to choose our president, our senators, and our representatives. During President Diem's tenure, with our own army, we were able to hold back every attempted invasion by the northern Communists.

From 1954 to at least 1963, we stopped the Communists at the border and never gave up one inch of our land. We never asked America to send troops to help us in protecting our newly built, free world. It was only after 1963, after President Diem's assassination when the American government decided to send troops to Vietnam, that we ran into more serious trouble. The Communists in the north, under the banner of "fighting the occupying Americans," quickly gained the sympathy of the world, including many Americans. The situation escalated until the time came that the American president withdrew U. S. troops in order to appease the American populace. President Nixon, with Henry Kissinger's assistance, rushed to sign the treaty in Paris, which indirectly handed the South to the Vietnamese Communists.[1]

---

1   Foreseeing the disaster that the Paris' cease-fire treaty would bring to his country, Mr. Nguyen Van Thieu, then President of the Republic of Viet Nam, was reluctant to sign it. President Richard Nixon told his national security adviser, Henry Kissinger, that he had to get Thieu to sign the treaty, and that he would "cut off

The Southern Vietnamese army suddenly found itself alone in the fight to stop the spread of Communism. Nevertheless, our soldiers held on and did not accept defeat until our last president, President Duong Van Minh, ordered them to surrender - two years after all American troops withdrawn, and when U.S. Congress cut all aid to Vietnam. The South, without the support of the U. S., did not have the resources or arms to fight. Our soldiers had fought to protect our freedom for 21 years and were not about to give it up so easily.

For the sake of all of the Americans who have been sent to Iraq to fight the war launched by this administration, I will pray for a Secretary of Defense who is better informed and a better student of history. We already have more than enough trouble with a President who doesn't like to read books.

Hoang Duoc Thao

(Publisher and Editor of *The Little Saigon News*)

(Thieu's) head if necessary". Nixon's verbal statement was caught on tape. (News York Times news service-June 24, 2009)

11

SECRETARY OF DEFENSE DONALD H. RUMSFELD

Not only does the Secretary of Defense have a poor knowledge of the Vietnam War, he apparently doesn't even see clearly the current history of Iraq war.

On December 8, 2004, Secretary Rumsfeld came to Buehring camp in Kuwait to encourage the soldiers before sending them into Iraq. At the end of his speech, he was surprised by questions from some of the young Americans who were about to face the deadly dangers of the battlefield.

Eric Schmitt, of *The New York Times*, described the unexpected scene:

Spc. Thomas Wilson, a scout with a Tennessee National Guard unit scheduled to roll into Iraq this week, was the first to step forward, saying that soldiers had to scrounge through local landfills for pieces of rusty scrap metal and bulletproof glass — what they called "hillbilly armor" — to bolt to their trucks.

"Why don't we have those resources readily available to us?" Wilson asked Rumsfeld, drawing cheers and applause from many of the 2,300 soldiers assembled in a hangar.

A few minutes later, a soldier from the Idaho National Guard's 116th Armor Cavalry Brigade asked Rumsfeld what he and the Army were doing "to address shortages and antiquated equipment" that will affect National Guard soldiers heading to Iraq.

The soldiers of a superpower's army had *"to scrounge through local landfills for pieces of rusty scrap metal… to bolt to their trucks."* That sounded absurd. At first, Secretary Rumsfeld was surprised, nearly speechless. Then he felt annoyed, may be a little embarrassed. "Now, settle down, settle down, Hell, I'm an old man, it's early in the morning, and I'm gathering my thoughts here," he said.

When Mr. Rumsfeld has settled himself down and gathered all his thoughts, he said he had no doubt that army leaders were providing the newest and best equipment to the troops headed for combat.

That was all the comfort the soldiers would hear from their boss.

"If you think about it, you can have all the armor in the world on a tank and a tank can be blown up, and you can have an up-armored Humvee and it can be blown up," Mr. Rumsfeld remarked defensively.

Not much encouragement there! Our Secretary of Defense had just pointed out to American soldiers that they had a very slim chance of survival in the near future, since all the armor in the world cannot save them from being blown up.

As if punishing his troops with such hopeless reality were not enough, Secretary Rumsfeld went even further. *"You go to war with the army you have, not the army you might want or wish to have at a later time,"* he said.

Here Mr. Rumsfeld exaggerated the soldiers' request and tried to put them in their place. They were not asking for a better army to go to war with. They just needed the Secretary of Defense to take responsibility, do his job, by relieving them from *"scrounge through local landfills"* by sending them into the battlefield with better equipment than *"pieces of rusty scrap metal and bulletproof glass."*

Obviously, Secretary Rumsfeld failed to lift the morale of his troops. The American soldiers didn't deserve such a verbal attack. But even though the Secretary's mean-spirited defense might create a negative, unsettling feeling among the troops, the greater danger appeared in his obvious ignorance of the pathetic state of affairs with regard to the soldiers' equipment and supplies.

He didn't know that his soldiers struggled with a lack of armor, and protective gear, vehicles and equipment. And he had no clue about our soldiers' adventures on the landfills!

He hadn't seen something that many Americans, especially those whose children have been sent to Iraq, had seen.

Once these Americans recognized the problem, they used their own money to rectify it. Some parents dug into their own pockets, while the poorer ones got together in small groups to raise funds. They bought bulletproof jackets, and other gear, which was sent to the battlefields to protect American troops. They quietly performed the job of Secretary Rumsfeld and the Pentagon.

"Your expectation is that when you are sent to war, that our government does everything they can do to protect the lives of our people, and anything less than that is not good enough," said a former Marine who spent nearly $1,000 two weeks ago to buy lower-body armor for his son, a Marine serving in Fallujah.

The father asked that he be identified only by his first name — Gordon — because he fears retribution against his son. (Lolita C. Baldor-AP)

Some parents even buy better weapons. The father of Marine Sgt. Todd Bowers bought his son a high-tech riflescope for $600 and a $100 pair of goggles that actually saved his life.

Not only the parents and relatives cared about our soldiers. In Jan. 2005, Acting Governor of New Jersey Richard Codey asked all local, state and federal law enforcement agencies to donate used vests that could be used to strengthen armor on military vehicles. Senator Christopher Dodd, of Connecticut, got involved by recommending that Congress request that the Pentagon reimburse those who bought military equipments with their own money. He said that men and women in uniform "shouldn't have to rely on bake sales and lemonade stands to raise money" to get them the equipment they need (AP).

Why didn't Secretary Rumsfeld know about some of the U.S. army's problems whereas Senator Dodd, Acting Governor Codey, and the American people know about them very well? I afraid the answer would be: he has been too busy to read the newspapers.

I guess he didn't even have the time to glance at the photos published with the war news. Because if he had spent a little time observing these photos, he would have encountered one published by the AP in December 2004 which shows two Marines tying sandbags on a piece of plywood laid over the top of their vehicle, with the following caption: "U.S. military personnel in Iraq have had to improvise because of the armor shortage. Marines prepared a vehicle with plywood and sandbags before last month's assault on Fallujah." Then he would have known how vulnerable our soldiers actually were when facing the enemy's weapons, especially the roadside bombs. And he wouldn't have been surprised and irritated by questions about what he has done and will do to make their missions more achievable and less deadly.

There were more victims of our poorly informed Secretary of Defense. On August 28, 2006, Rumsfeld said the following at the Fallon Naval Air Station, Nev.: "They (the terrorists) are actively manipulating the media in this country" by, for example, falsely blaming U.S. troops for civilian deaths in Iraq and Afghanistan, he said. "They can lie with impunity," he said, while U.S. troops are held to a high standard of conduct," and "...That's the thing that keeps me up at night... What bothers me the most is how clever the enemy is." (Robert Burns – AP)

So over three years into the war, Secretary Rumsfeld apparently still had no clue about Iraqi and Afghan civilians being killed by American troops, albeit unintentionally. He thought that the stories of civilians being killed were a product of the terrorists' propaganda that a gullible American media was blindly buying as the truth.

As of the day Secretary Rumsfeld delivered those remarks, the President of Afghanistan, Hamid Karzai, had complained several times about the U.S.- led coalition forces killing many civilians and causing outrage among his people, creating huge problem for his administration. And even as Mr. Rumsfeld spoke, a group of U.S. Marines had been arrested on suspicion of killing 24 Iraqi civilians at Haditha in November 2005 and five other Marines were suspected of committing a horrible crime in Mahmoudiya: They were accused of raping a 14 year-old Iraqi girl, burning her body, and killing her parents and sister!

The media had been widely reporting the details of these cases for months. But since Secretary Rumsfeld believes that all the incidents weren't real, but only lies passed on by a media which was being manipulated by the terrorists, he still confidently denied their existence.

Not only was there solid evidence in the news but on the Pentagon's budget sheet as well. The U.S. military in Iraq listed the dollar amount it would pay as compensation to families of innocent Iraqi civilians killed or wounded by U.S. forces. Injured Iraqis were paid from $500 to $1000, depending on the seriousness of the wound. The families of those killed received up to $2500 per one life. If the soldiers firing at a car killed the parents who left behind a bunch of kids with a totaled vehicle, the U.S. military would show their generosity by paying the children $7500 because the vehicle's life has the same dollar value of a human's.

By the time the Secretary of Defense was trying to convince the world that civilian killing only existed in the terrorists' propaganda, the Pentagon has already spent about thirty million dollars in payouts for the wounded or dead Iraqi civilians.

My Dear Commander- in- Chief,

If you were President George W. Bush and your Secretary of Defense were Donald Rumsfeld, you should, at this point, quickly give him the boot to prevent more harm being done to the Iraqis and American soldiers.

By not acknowledge civilian casualties, Secretary Rumsfeld could ignore a reality that would require taking appropriate actions for its resolution. Being totally ignorant about the soldiers' lack of equipment would render him a terribly incompetent Secretary of Defense unable to protect our soldiers on the battlefield or improving the power and the effectiveness of the American army.

And most of all, this country does not need a man, who instead of considering each soldier's life precious and highly valuing the ultimate sacrifice each of them, makes, throws into the soldiers' faces a cruel statement that all the armor in the world couldn't save them from being blown up!

No soldiers who are about to go to war deserved a Secretary of Defense who hides his ignorance and incompetence behind tough, abusive and insulting language.

12

Torture

Besides the well-known techniques of abusing terrorist suspects-waterboarding, forced nudity, severe sleep deprivation, extended confinement in small, dark boxes, etc, which are techniques used by the Chinese communist during the Korean War to obtain mostly false confessions from U.S. prisoners – if you were a Republican Commander-in-Chief, a big fan of former Vice President Dick Cheney, and supporting his "interrogation policy," you should be aware of another kind of "enhanced interrogation" made in America and practiced under President Bush's watch.

On Feb. 10, 2005, reporting on the content of former Army translator Erik Saar's book (not yet to be published at that time) Carol D. Leonnig and Dana Priest of the *Washington Post* wrote that female American interrogators had tortured detainees by debasing their own bodies: "Female interrogators repeatedly used sexually suggestive tactics to try to humiliate and pry information from devout Muslim men held at the U.S. military prison at Guantanamo Bay, Cuba, according to a military investigation not yet made public and newly declassified accounts from detainees."

And here is one scene of our interrogators in action:

German detainee Murat Kurnaz told his lawyer that three women in lacy bras and panties strutted into the interrogation room where he was sitting in chains. They cooed about how attractive he was and suggested "they could have some fun," he said.

When Kurnaz averted his eyes, he said, one woman sat on his lap, another rubbed her breasts against his back and massaged his chest and a third squatted near his crotch.

Paisley Dodds of the AP described a scenario based on the same document: "One female civilian contractor used a special outfit that included a miniskirt, thong underwear and a bra during late-night interrogations with prisoners, mostly Muslim men who consider it taboo to have close contact with women who aren't their wives… Some Guantanamo prisoners who have been released say they were tormented by 'prostitutes'."

I assume the designer of this torture technique was a man, one who saw no harm in asking female soldiers and associated civilians to degrade themselves to illicit answers from detainees. Or is he actually a wise guy who just wanted to add a little fun to his routine job? I suppose that while the detainees were confused and tormented by the female interrogators, the author and his male colleagues watching nearby were enjoying the show themselves.

Did this technique bother his superiors? Not much apparently. A senior Pentagon official said that the military does not condone "sexual activity" during interrogations, but that good interrogators *"take initiative and are a little creative."*

So the inventors of these morally degrading interrogation tactics were just being a "little creative" and there is nothing to worry about.

But the "creative" interrogators didn't stop there. Besides exploiting their sexuality, some female interrogators even went as far as using their own natural biological makeup as way to frighten and intimidate, and thus pry information and confessions from the Muslim male detainees.

The interrogator left the room to ask a Muslim linguist how she could break the prisoner's reliance on God. The linguist told her to tell the detainee that she was menstruating, touch him, then make sure to turn off the water in his cell so he couldn't wash.

Strict interpretation of Islamic law forbids physical contact with any menstruating women, who are considered unclean.

"The concept was to make the detainee feel that after talking to her he was unclean and was unable to go before his God in prayer and gain strength," says the draft, stamped *"Secret."*

"The interrogator used ink from a red pen to fool the detainee," Saar wrote. *"She then started to place her hands in her pants as she walked behind the detainee,"* he wrote. *"As she circled around him he could see that she was taking her hand out of her pants. When it became visible the detainee saw what appeared to be red blood on her hand. She said, 'Who sent you to Arizona?' He then glared at her with a piercing look of hatred."*

"She then wiped the red ink on his face. He shouted at the top of his lungs, spat at her and lunged forward – so fiercely that he broke loose from one ankle shackle." (Paisley Dodds, AP)

Mamdouh Habib, an Australian man released from Guantanamo Bay last month, said he was strapped down while a woman told him she was "menstruating" on his face. (Carol D. Leonnig and Dana Priest, WP)

Yet, was this the limit of humiliation and perversion that the interrogators might inflict on these Muslim prisoners? No, there was one more step, one that could be deemed the climax of this technique. That was to insult their religious faith by abusing the Koran.

Newsweek magazine, in May 2005, wrote that during interrogations, U.S. guards had flushed a Koran down a toilet trying to provoke detainees into talking. That revelation led to violent protest demonstrations in Pakistan and Afghanistan where 17 people died and several were wounded.

The Pentagon immediately blamed… *Newsweek* for inciting the anger of the Muslim world. Officials denied that the toilet incident ever happened, and said that *Newsweek* reporter Michael Isikoff had failed to perform his job responsibly. Bryan Whitman, a Pentagon spokesman, accused *Newsweek* of causing damage to America's reputation: "Newsweek hid behind anonymous sources, which by their own admission do not withstand scrutiny. Unfortunately, they cannot retract the damage they have done to this nation or those that were viciously attacked by those false allegations."

"False allegations"? Mark Whitaker, *Newsweek*'s editor, didn't think so. He wrote in reply: "We regret that we got any part of our story wrong, and extend our sympathies to victims of the violence and to the U.S. soldiers caught in its midst," but, during an interview, he affirmed that *Newsweek* would make no retraction, adding "We don't know what the ultimate facts are."

Whitaker had good reason to stand his ground. He had a *star witness* - three stars, in fact - who unintentionally backed up his argument. At a Pentagon news conference on May 15, answering reporters' questions about the allegation, Gen. Richard B. Myers, Chairman of the Joint Chiefs of Staff, said that military investigators at Guantánamo were searching their interrogation logs to find the case cited in the *Newsweek* article.

"They have looked through the logs, the interrogation logs, and they cannot confirm yet that there were ever the case of the toilet incident, *except for one case, a log entry, which they still have to confirm, where a detainee was reported by a guard to be ripping pages out of a Koran and putting in the toilet to stop it up as a protest,*" he said. "But not where the U.S. did it."

So, Gen. Myers confirmed the existence of an incident in which a Koran – whether the whole thing or just a few pages – was put in a toilet. The question here was who did it. According to the guard's log entry, a detainee, not any U.S. interrogator, committed the crime. And so, if we believe the guard's version is credible and truthful, a detainee himself ripped pages out of a Koran and stuffed them in a toilet.

On June 3, 2005, The Pentagon released the findings of its investigation into allegations that the Koran had been mishandled. The report stated that, in fact, American personnel were at fault on several occasions. The inquiry found that in about five confirmed cases, interrogators or guards kicked, stepped on, and intentionally or *"accidentally"* splashed urine on the Koran.

Apparently, many U.S. interrogators and guards — including the *"good and creative"* ones — have mixed up physical torture with psychological and moral humiliation on the assumption that it will produce the same fruits. They do not know that humiliation and insult only hurt the victims' feelings, usually inciting more hatred and anger in them. Instead of cooperating or surrendering, the victims sometimes react violently. *"Murat Kurnaz head-butted the woman behind him…"* *"The detainee spat in her face…"* Another detainee shouted and *"lunged forward – so fiercely that he broke loose from one ankle shackle."*

*

As Commander-in-Chief, you should make sure that no members of our armed forces ever again have to participate in such disgusting interrogation tactics. As a decent human being, you should wish that no one in the world would be treated as some of the detainees were at Guantánamo or be exposed to any kind of torture anywhere.

You should order that interrogators and guards be closely supervised while performing their duty, to be sure they follow the rule of law at all times, and be truthful in their reports. And their supervisor should use intelligent curiosity and common sense.

I afraid Gen. Richard B. Myers doesn't qualify for that supervisory position. The guard's log entry reporting that a detainee himself ripped pages out of a Koran and put them in a toilet didn't bother him, or raise any suspicion. Apparently, he trusted the integrity and honesty of the entry's author. He brought the guard's story to the public, treating it as an undisputed fact.

Before talking to the media, Gen. Myers should have asked himself: Was there any Muslim in Guantanamo, or anyone among billion Muslim men and women in the world, who would disrespect the Koran to the point that he or she was willing to rip off its pages and *"[put them in] the toilet to stop it up as a protest"*?

And what was this man's alleged target of protest? Was he protesting the U.S. soldiers' desecration of his Koran?

13

EDUCATIONAL WAR NEWS

There is a cheap training our military can use that will certainly improve its chance for success. And it would save lives and America's reputation, too.

In preparing the future generation of military leaders, the Commander-in-Chief should order all cadets of the U.S. military academies to read select war news. This would not be done individually, but together in class or in groups where the instructor would introduce the news with current educational themes.

At the end, they should draw the best lessons that those small historical war incidents can offer.

Following are some examples:

News Story #1

About four months into the war in Iraq, on August 3, 2003, Shaila K. Dewan of the *New York Times* wrote this statement: *"After the war, American soldiers referred to Iraqi looters as 'Ali Babas.' Now, the name is more commonly used by Iraqis to describe the soldiers."*

The reason, Dewan said, was that many Iraqis believed that the U.S. soldiers came here to rob them of money, jewelry and cars.

On any given day, Iraqis can be found pleading at the gates of military bases or in civil affairs offices: an old woman who laments that her savings were taken from her son on the road to Baghdad; a young man who says he gave a Thuraya phone to a soldier for a call and did not get it back; a cigarette merchant who says he returned to a checkpoint to recover his car the day after it was confiscated, only to find that both car and checkpoint had vanished.

"I always used to have the radio by my ear just waiting for when the Americans come here," said Ruslia Rumdhan Niima, who was on her fifth trip to Baghdad from the countryside to search for the 7 million dinars she claims Americans took from her son. "Now that they came, this is what happens."

Assad Ibrahim Mehdi, a vegetable seller, is one of the few complainants who can muster a witness. That person, a military translator, has signed an affidavit attesting that during a raid in April, soldiers took the family's savings - about $2,000 in dinars - and an old tin chocolate box containing the deed to his family's house, their citizenship papers and their ration card. The soldiers left no receipt, and Mr. Mehdi considers his property stolen. "What else would you call it?" he said on a recent day, after waiting three hours in the sun to see a soldier about his complaint...

Why did the U.S. soldiers behave no better than "Ali Babas"?

Part of the problem is a cultural misunderstanding. In Iraq's cash-based society, it is not unusual for people to carry stacks of dinars and a gun to protect them. But soldiers who discovered piles of cash (a million dinars equals only $700) and an AK-47 often assumed the owner was up to no good.

Even now, some soldiers seem not to realize that many Iraqis are carrying on their business - buying houses, selling cars and livestock - often in cash.

"Where would an Iraqi get $3,000?" one sergeant asked when the question of confiscation was raised. "I can't even get $3,000." Dewan wrote.

American military officials said that in most instances property believed stolen was more likely to have been confiscated during raids or at checkpoints. So where were those confiscated items and money going?

Trips to the airport, where evidence is supposed to be stored, have turned up sunglasses, prayer beads, ID's and car keys. Impounded cars have been towed to lots all over Baghdad. Some items, the civil affairs officers said, wind up as souvenirs - one American Humvee has been seen sporting an odd relic: an upside-down Iraqi license plate.

"The checkpoints made a routine practice of confiscating large sums of money," said Sgt. First Class James Pratt. "But they did not follow the proper chain of the evidentiary process."... *"Even if the soldiers involved can be identified, chances are they have already been shipped out of the country"* (with the evidence, a large sums of money, probably?).

Sgt. Thad Farlow, a civil affairs officer whose unit runs a civilian assistance center, said the complaints he heard stemmed from a mixture of negligence and actual misconduct. "It's kind of hard to win the hearts and minds when soldiers are taking $650 Thuraya phones," he said, referring to a type of satellite telephone.

The reactions of the Iraqis surprised no one:

Iraqi community leaders warn that the perception is poisoning Iraqi attitudes, buttressing a sense of powerlessness and creating opposition to the American-led occupation, even among Iraqis who welcomed the ouster of Saddam Hussein.

But the American forces have done little to refute the rumors of theft. Nor is there a centralized system to help Iraqis recover their property or to answer Iraqi complaints.

So the notion that the liberators turned out to be "Ali Babas" *"is flickering through the capital, propelled by word of mouth and amplified by anti-Western elements ready to exploit any hint of American misbehavior."*

Here is what this news was telling me:

The Iraqis had good reason to believe that U.S. soldiers, at the checkpoints or conducting raids, were bunch of crooks. Some actually were. They kept the Iraqis' money and used their property as souvenirs. They appeared much more dangerous to the society than Ali Baba, who was only a thief. These men were behaving like the armed bandits or those bad apples in law enforcement who commit robberies under the color of authority.

Some soldiers were simply ignorant. They had no clue about the cash-based society that exists all over the world. They thought the Iraqis, like Americans, would mostly carry on their business with checks, credit cards, etc... rather than cash. So anyone who goes around carrying large sum of money should be treated as a criminal suspect.

Some soldiers were not only ignorant but also arrogant, like the sergeant who believed that since he himself was unable to have three thousand dollars, no one among twenty five million Iraqis could honestly possess that large amount of money.

But we cannot blame the soldiers alone for creating this ugly mess. They were all following the orders of their leaders, who were probably just as ignorant and arrogant.

Military officials wrote the army's manual for the soldiers to learn from, setting up rules and regulations, providing the lists of do's and don'ts at checkpoints and during raids. They instructed the soldiers how to act, react and treat civilians in the field, including teaching them some essential culture of the occupied country.

As one official said, *" property believed stolen was more likely to have been confiscated during raids or at checkpoints,"* which implies that besides some irregular cases of missing money and property stemming from *"a mixture of negligence and actual misconduct,"* the soldiers' confiscation was part of their duty dictated by their leaders or by military policy.

Those U.S. soldiers who followed regulations surrendered all the seized money and property to the evidence storage. Impounded cars were towed to lots all over Baghdad. Most confiscated items were stored at the airport, where the victims of checkpoints and raids could find their sunglasses, prayer beads, IDs and car keys. So any improperly seized item showing up at the storeroom would be constitute strong evidence of the soldiers' misconduct.

But apparently, the military officials in Iraq were not bothered by the reports of prayer beads, car keys, IDs, jewelry, an old tin chocolate box containing the deed to one family's house, citizenship papers, ration cards and money being confiscated from Iraqi civilians.

And what happened to the large sums of money that never reached the evidence room? Did they go into the pockets of the soldiers or did some find its way into the wallets of some corrupted officers?

The Iraqis couldn't care less about who would enjoy their money and property. To them, they were all Americans, the occupiers. The story of the occupiers acting as thieves and robbers flickered not only through the capital but also throughout the country. The insurgents loved it, made sure every Iraqi found out about it.

That knowledge might have led some Iraqis to their deaths.

At that time, there were several incidents at checkpoints in which Iraqi families riding in cars were shot at, and all or most of the family members were killed. The shooters explained that the driver, instead of stopping the car as ordered, had made a U-turn to evade the checkpoints, acting very suspicious, like terrorists.

Some survivors explained that they did not understand the hand signals and verbal orders of the U.S. soldiers. Others said they made the U-turn because they were afraid if they continued through the checkpoints, the women in the car, especially their daughters, would be inappropriately touched by the soldiers performing body searches.

I wonder if there might be another reason:

Perhaps the driver had made U-turn to avoid going through the checkpoint where he believed his family would be robbed by armed-to-the-teeth American Ali Babas.

And this non-fiction story might result in the deaths of who knows how many U.S. troops, too.

Shortly after the invasion, the Iraqis found they had lost the freedom of moving around the city, and while going through American checkpoints, their right to possess sunglasses, cars, prayer beads, jewelry and money no longer existed. And if they avoided going out, and just stayed home, avoiding the dangers of passing through checkpoints, their money and property were still not safe. Ali Babas could conduct a raid and come to their home to get them anyway.

Many Iraqis would be willing to join the insurgents to fight back.

So the U.S. troops shot at the cars of Iraqi families turning away from checkpoints because they wrongly identified them as terrorists. And the Iraqis who joined the insurgency were willing to die to kill the American soldiers because they mistook the liberators for bandits who, they thought, came here to liberate no one but only to rob them of money, jewelry and cars.

A tragic case of mistaken identity… of our own creation!

News Story #2

WASHINGTON — *The Pentagon has assigned the task of tracking down and eliminating Osama bin Laden, Saddam Hussein and other high-*

profile targets to an Army general who sees the war on terrorism as a clash between Judeo-Christian values and Satan.

Lt. Gen. William G. "Jerry" Boykin, the new deputy undersecretary of Defense for intelligence, is a much-decorated and twice-wounded veteran of covert military operations. From the bloody 1993 clash with Muslim warlords in Somalia chronicled in "Black Hawk Down" and the hunt for Colombian drug czar Pablo Escobar to the ill-fated attempt to rescue American hostages in Iran in 1980, Boykin was in the thick of things.

Yet the former commander and 13-year veteran of the Army's top-secret Delta Force is also an outspoken evangelical Christian who appeared in dress uniform and polished jump boots before a religious group in Oregon in June to declare that radical Islamists hated the United States "because we're a Christian nation, because our foundation and our roots are Judeo-Christian ... and the enemy is a guy named Satan."

Discussing the battle against a Muslim warlord in Somalia, Boykin told another audience, "I knew my God was bigger than his. I knew that my God was a real God and his was an idol."

"We in the army of God, in the house of God, kingdom of God have been raised for such a time as this," Boykin said last year.

On at least one occasion, in Sandy, Ore., in June, Boykin said of President Bush: "He's in the White House because God put him there" (Richard T. Cooper of the *Los Angeles Times*- 10.2003)

Since the first day of the Iraq occupation, President Bush has labored to convince the Islamic world that the U.S. Forces' sole purpose is to democratize Iraq, spreading freedom and democracy throughout the Middle East. The Islamic extremists, the insurgents, however, refused to believe in any American President's good intention or noble cause. They always accused the Americans of being the Christian crusaders who are once again attempting to invade Islamic nations.

The debate went on and we begun gaining ground because most people in the world, while they may disagree with our policies and tactics, did not believe that America wanted to start a religious war in the 21st Century.

Then suddenly, an American general announces that the U.S. military is an army of a bigger God, putting a religious face on the war, and giving a great deal of credibility to the other side's argument.

To his credit, Gen. Boykin apologized a few days later to those offended by his statements and said he never meant to offend Muslims. But the damage was hard to control from our side at this point.

Since three-star general Boykin is the Pentagon's Deputy Undersecretary of Defense for intelligence, his words were quickly interpreted by our enemies as the policy of the U.S. government. The Muslim militants have usually treated all American civilian or military officials' statements as seriously as the President's. (Actually, many of our own people are no different. They hear an Islamist senior cleric cite a passage from the Quran that orders death to all "infidels," or a terrorist leader threaten that Islamic nations will soon conquer and rule the whole world… and they quickly become suspicious of all the Muslims.)

Armed with the new-found legitimacy of their holy war, the Islamic extremists would likely be able to speed up their recruitment and reinforce their propaganda. Surely there are a huge number of young Muslims who are willing to die to prove their God is real and big.

Boykin's statements will probably bring him only some uncomfortable moments with his superiors and the bother of issuing an apology. But it certainly will create many more determined martyrs for our soldiers to deal with.

News Story #3

Excerpts from a report by Rick Rogers of the *San Diego- Union-Tribune* (February 4, 2005):

A Marine Corps general with ties to Camp Pendleton has sparked global debate by saying "It's fun to shoot some people" and poking fun at the manhood of Afghans during a speech Tuesday in San Diego.

Lt. Gen. James Mattis made his comments at the San Diego Convention Center amid an exposition sponsored by the U.S. Naval Institute and the Armed Forces Communications and Electronics Association.

A career infantry officer, Mattis until recently commanded the 1st Marine Division at Camp Pendleton. Now stationed in Quantico, Va., he is in charge of developing better ways to train and equip Marines…

On Tuesday, Mattis responded to a question about fighting Iraqi insurgents by saying: "Actually, it's a lot of fun to fight. You know, it's a hell of a hoot. … It's fun to shoot some people. I'll be right up front with you, I like brawling…"

...Mattis went on to take a not-so-subtle poke at the purported treatment of women in the Middle East.

He said: "You go into Afghanistan, you got guys who slap women around for five years because they didn't wear a veil. You know, guys like that ain't got no manhood left anyway. So it's a hell of a lot of fun to shoot them..."

...The Council on American-Islamic Relations, a Muslim civil liberties group, called on the Pentagon to discipline Mattis for his comments.

"We do not need generals who treat the grim business of war as a sporting event," said the council's executive director, Nihad Awad. "These disturbing remarks are indicative of an apparent indifference to the value of human life..."

Gen. Mattis enjoys brawling, and thinks fighting is a lot of fun. That may not be unusual, perhaps even beneficial for a career in military. His remarks, though controversial and not appropriate for a U.S. general, violated no military rules and regulations and are protected by the law of the land.

However, if he finds it "a hell of a lot of fun" to shoot a Afghanistan man who have "no manhood", or just shoot anyone, his mentality is dangerously similar to that of a serial killer, who kills to satisfy his sadistic pleasure.

I sincerely hope that Gen. Mattis hasn't lost his mind and that he does not really find it a lot of fun to shoot a human being. He might be exaggerating his enthusiasm to inspire American youngsters, encouraging them to join the Marines. And it's not a bad tactic – though immoral — for recruitment since millions American teenagers already have fun killing, shooting at human beings and everything else, in scores of popular video games. They might be excited by Mattis's statement. He knows his target audience very well.

Would Gen. Mattis's speech damage the U.S. armed forces' reputation by bringing into the Marine Corps a bunch of serial killers? I hope not. There are not many men with sick minds out there. And this kind of killer has usually sought satisfaction by many other ways besides joining the Army.

Upon reaching the age to enlist, the teenagers, who had fun shooting at virtual people, would be old enough to realize that the battlefield isn't as safe as a game room, and their targets shoot back with real bullets. Apparently, Gen. Mattis had done no harm to America.

The danger in his remarks, like those of Gen. Boykin, lies in their effect on the enemy.

We — American youngsters included — may not take Mattis's words seriously. But the Afghans, Iraqis and those of culturally related countries will. They may be guilty of forcing their women to wear veils, and thus losing their manhood and deserving death, according to judge Mattis's opinion.

Terrorist organizations and insurgent leaders will use Gen. Mattis's statement as a great tool to recruit new members who believe that American soldiers come to their country to kill them for fun, because they are not worthy to live.

Like Gen. Boykin's statement, Mattis's remarks will produce many more determined, formidable fighters willing to blow themselves up to fight the invaders who "kill for fun".

News Story # 4

In Sept. 2004, U.S. forces were about to surround and attack insurgents in Fallujah, a stronghold of Sunni Muslim rebels.

Lt. Gen. Thomas F. Metz, America's leader number two commander in Iraq, announced his strategy:

The U.S. military, he said, will work to regain control of rebel strongholds and turn them over to Iraq's fledgling security forces so elections will be seen by Iraqis- and the world- as free and fair…

Assaults to retake these areas could be done consecutively or simultaneously, Metz said. He said one or more might be solved through negotiations, with leaders warning that their cities face a devastating U.S. offensive if the insurgents don't stand down.

"If you're a leader in a town… do you want to have to go rebuild it because it got destroyed, because foreign fighters came to hang out in your city? They can help us make these decisions," Metz said. (Jim Krane of the AP)

One month later, in Oct. 2004, apparently inspired by the American general's tactics, Ayad Allawi, then Iraqi Prime Minister, required the Fallujah people to perform an even harder task: turning in the Al-Qaeda leader and his group in exchange for the cessation of attacks by Iraqi military and the U.S. forces.

"If they do not turn in al-Zarqawi (al Qaeda-leader) and his group, we will carry out operations in Fallujah," Prime Minister Ayad Allawi told a

meeting of the 100-member interim National Council. "Fallujah of course is an honest city, but it has been manipulated by a deviant bunch that wants to harm Iraq." (Nadia Abou el-Magd of the AP)

Gen. Metz was absolutely right on one thing: A town's leaders don't want to have their homes destroyed by the U.S. forces. They don't want to have to bury the town citizens, victims of a devastating American offensive, either.

But demanding them to force the insurgents to stand down, or, as Prime Minister Allawi required, to capture and turn in an al-Qaeda leader and his group, is assigning them a mission impossible.

A robber with a gun can control and dictate the movements, and even the fates, of dozens people inside a bank, including the bank's manager. It is ridiculous for us to ask this leader of the bank to handcuff the robber and turn him over to the police.

So even in the best scenario if the insurgents were only a small group of *"foreign fighters who came to hang out in the city,"* or *"a deviant bunch that wants to harm Iraq,"* they were still extremely dangerous, and not easily captured.

In Fallujah at that time, the insurgents had the entire town as their hostage. They ruled. They made the decisions on jailing or killing the city folks, not vice versa.

The negotiation tactics of Gen. Metz and P.M. Allawi indirectly handed the leader and citizens of Fallujah a death sentence. Refuse to turn in the rebels and their city would be destroyed, and many would be killed. But should they try to subdue and arrest the armed-to-teeth-insurgents, they would meet Death quicker.

*

*　　*

The four examples above offer precious lessons among the dozens that could be given to the cadets. They teach them early in their military career to be aware of the damage and danger an irresponsible statement can inflict on U.S. Forces' reputation and the safety of its soldiers, and the destruction and lost in civilian lives that an ill-conceived strategy can cause.

These cadets will be our military leaders, and in time, some may make general, Secretary of Defense, and perhaps even Commander-in-Chief.

14

FIGHTING THERE OR FIGHTING HERE

In August 2003, Lt. Gen. Ricardo Sanchez, the newly assigned commander of the U.S. forces in Iraq, told D'Arcy Doran of the Associated Press that the attacks on American troops were coming from a variety of sources.

"Clearly I think it's the former regime loyalists and the foreign fighters-slash-terrorists. Those are my two top priorities right now… the groups have very selfish interests…It's to re-establish their own power base so they can continue with the repressive controls they used to have on this country,"

And Gen. Sanchez firmly cautioned the American people:

"Every American needs to believe this: that if we fail here in this environment, the next battlefield will be the streets of America."

Listening to Gen. Sanchez's advice, as an American, I just hoped that he knew better what he was doing than what he was saying.

This type of comment is usually reserved for the President. I would expect him, as a new arrival to Iraq assuming the role of military leader, to inform Americans about his assessment of the situation, and, if possible, what his plan was for pacifying Iraq. Gen. Ricardo Sanchez should've left the propaganda to the civilian leadership.

He should also focus more attention on identifying the enemies. The list he provided was poor and dangerously inadequate.

Even though at that time the anti-American Shiite groups of cleric Muqtada al-Sadr — who was never a regime loyalist and had wanted Saddam Hussein overthrown — hasn't yet come on stage, every general should know that, throughout the history of war, occupation has been met with resistance. More important, a few months before Sanchez's arrival, Paul Bremer, the top U.S. civilian administrator in Iraq, had created a huge number of enemies for American troops by ordering the dissolution of the Iraqi armed forces and several security bodies. Driven by a sense of honor, dignity and patriotism, they would be willing to fight against the occupiers, and Gen. Sanchez shouldn't have ignored those formidable groups of enemies.

Even if Sanchez's enemy list was accurate and complete, his warning still doesn't make sense. It's hard to believe that the former regime's loyalists and the foreign fighters/terrorists, if left unchecked, would invade the streets of America. Especially the "foreign terrorists", if they wanted to attack America why would they have to wait until American forces failed to defeat them in Iraq first?

Sanchez wants us to believe that the occupation of Iraq is preventing terrorists from reaching American soil. Does he mean that had we attacked and occupied Iraq before 9/11, bin Laden's terrorists would have been too busy fighting American troops in Iraq to go and fly planes into the Twin Towers and the Pentagon?

I don't believe Sanchez's statement, and apparently President Bush didn't either in the period before the invasion. In fact, just twenty-four hours before ordering the invasion, Mr. Bush said that if Saddam Hussein and his two sons left the country, the war would not happen. Had Saddam accepted that condition, President Bush wouldn't have to send U.S. troops into Iraq at all. He might be very surprised by Sanchez's imagined future Iraqi enemies who would come to attack on American soil.

But that was the pre-Iraq war President George W. Bush, whose modest goal at the time was simply to remove Saddam Hussein from power. After that, the President and his administration have repeatedly used Sanchez's warning as a grave threat to scare the American people into supporting an open-ended occupation.

Paul Bremer was more specific, "I would rather be fighting them here [Iraq] than fighting them in New York." The President uses the horrible picture of "fighting in the streets of America" to terrify any one who doubts his judgment and wisdom. Mr. Bush repeated this warning in several interviews "If we leave (Iraq), *they will follow us here.*" (Daniel Henninger/*Wall Street Journal.* Oct. 27, 2006.) "The operative phrase that I thought made a lot of sense about this war is: *if we fail in Iraq, the enemy will follow us here.*" (Scott Pelley/ *60 Minutes* Jan. 12, 2007.)

His statement quickly provided good material for comedians and late night talk show hosts. On *The Daily Show*, Jon Stewart asked his guest Dr. Zbigniew Brzezinski, the former national security adviser for President Jimmy Carter, by what mean Iraqi terrorists would cross an ocean following the withdrawal U.S. troops, as President Bush has often warned? "They'll swim!" Mr. Brzezinski answered.

Besides becoming a laughingstock, The President's threat embarrassed British Prime Minister Tony Blair.

In July 2005, just one week after a major terrorist attack in London, President Bush reminded everyone in his weekly radio address that American men and women were fighting in Iraq to prevent the terrorists from attacking us here.

Fortunately for Mr. Blair by then no one cared much what Mr. Bush had to say. However if Mr. Bush's words had reached the U.K., an angry media in London might have jumped on the Prime Minister, hammering him with these questions:

"The President of the U.S. says that he sent Americans to Iraq to prevent terrorist attack in New York, so how come you, Mr. Prime Minister, also sent British troops to Iraq but cannot stop terrorists from attacking in the streets of London?"

"Do Britain's sacrifices in Iraq serve only one purpose: to protect the streets of America?"

15

KEEPING BUSH'S ANTI-TERROR TACTICS

Two days after Barack Obama's inauguration, Marc A. Thiessen, chief speechwriter for President Bush, published an article in *The Washington Post* encouraging the new President to continue all of Mr. Bush's anti-terrorism policies. Thiessen vigorously defended the incarceration of suspects on Guantanamo, interrogation tactics, and warrantless eavesdropping, threatening that if President Obama put an end to these and terrorists were to strike on American soil again, he would be held responsible and *"the Democratic Party could find itself unelectable for a generation."*

He also warned against withdrawing troops from Iraq sooner than President Bush's schedule, meaning that the U.S. should stay there until 2011 rather than leave in 16 months as the new President has promised. *"President Bush revealed intelligence that Osama bin Laden had told al-Qaeda leaders in Iraq to form a cell to conduct attacks inside the United States - then the surge drove them from their havens and set back those plans. If Obama allows al-Qaeda to regain its Iraqi havens, and the terrorists use them to strike our country, he will not be able to blame Bush,"* he wrote.

In this article, Mr. Thiessen has introduced to the readers a dimwitted Osama bin Laden conducting an unbelievable strategy that would conveniently justify America's occupation of Iraq. Instead of ordering al-Qaeda leaders somewhere else in the world to form cells to conduct attacks inside the United States, bin Laden chose to assign the task to al-Qaeda in Iraq, which was already fighting day and night the biggest war in the world at this time. (What's wrong with Pakistan where all the London suicide bombers had been trained, Mr. Terrorists Boss!?)

According to President Bush's intelligence, Iraq's Al-Qaeda leaders were idiots as well. Somehow they needed to be in Iraq in order to plan attacks against the U.S., and when the surge drove them from there, they were rendered harmless. And they apparently have to reconstitute bases in Iraq before they can start again. It seems they cannot function anywhere but inside Iraq! (Why not Pakistan, Afghanistan, Yemen, Algeria, etc...?)

Apparently Al-Qaeda is restricted by both location and time. Their window for forming cells and planning attacks is strictly limited to the time between President Obama's withdrawal, if it happens early, and President Bush's schedule. If the new administration takes Thiessen's advice and keeps our troops in Iraq until 2011, then al-Qaeda's ability to attack America will be eliminated.

In comparison to President Bush's terrorists who were unable to attack America because the occupation had kept them busy inside Iraq, Mr. Thiessen's terrorists are even more feckless.

One interesting consequence of Thiessen's article is that it has made me more sympathetic to the former president. I think I understand him better. Disconnected, poorly informed, and surrounded by advisors like Mr. Thiessen, it's obvious why his foreign policy was made up of delusions and fallacies that have led to ruin.

If you fell in the same situation as Mr. Bush's, it would be hard for you to avoid making an illogical statement that defies common sense – or as E. J. Dionne Jr. gently put it, *"not an argument that took the average citizen's intelligence seriously."*

But one could avoid repeating it. One way is by watching late-night talk shows. If you have no time to do that yourself, you could order your speechwriters to do so. The writers and hosts of those entertaining shows are intelligent enough to quickly detect the inappropriate and fallacious part of your statement, and are talented enough to ridicule it, often the same day. They may embarrass and annoy you most of the time. But do not take it personally. Just join millions of your fellow citizens who, after a hardworking day, enjoy some good laughs on your expense. (And if you really want it, you could have the last laugh. Compared to the dear prices that your citizens usually have to pay for your mistake, your "expense" is actually a… joke.)

Just laugh it off and thank the ones who are preventing you from repeating your mistakes.

16

What's This Suicide Bomber's Motive?

In Nov. 2005, Sajida al-Rishawi — whose photo shows her with an explosive belt wrapped around her body, a photo that appeared first on Jordanian TV then all over the world — tried and failed to detonate her belt inside a Jordanian hotel. Meanwhile, her husband and their accomplices succeeded in their suicide bombing, killing sixty people. Sajida al-Rishawi was arrested, tried and sentenced to death by hanging.

Who is Sajida al-Rishawi? What did she hope to accomplish by blowing herself up and killing others?

Since she is Iraqi and a resident of Fallujah, she may belong to a terrorist group that "can't stand the thought of a free and peaceful Iraq."

This would be in keeping with one explanation for terrorist activity made by our Commander-in-Chief. In Oct. 2003, in a nationally televised news conference, President Bush had identified this kind of terrorist and warned the American people: *"It is dangerous in Iraq... because there are people who can't stand the thought of a free and peaceful Iraq".* Or she might not care about peace, but just hate freedom in general, as President Bush observed again on Apr. 2, 2004: *"...a free Iraq is something that the terrorists fear. They hate freedom. They can't stand the thought of a free society."*

But perhaps terrorist Sajida al-Rishawi hates something else entirely.

She may have no problem enduring the hardship of living in a free and peaceful Iraq, but cannot stand the offensive manner in which Westerners live. "They hate our way of life," many American politicians have observed. They are not alone in noting this. After the July 2005 attack in London, the Queen of England, during a visit to the Royal London Hospital, explained to the victims and all of Britain that "… those who perpetrate these brutal acts against innocent people should know that they will not change *our way of life.*"

According to the U.K. Prime Minister and many world major leaders, however, this female terrorist's motive may have nothing to do with "a free and peaceful Iraq," "freedom," in general, or the Western "way of life." She may instead be the type of terrorist that has more diabolical ambitions, as suggested by Prime Minister Tony Blair, who, while attending G-8 Summit in Gleneagles, Scotland, read a joint statement of the leaders present, saying: "Today's bombings will not weaken in any way our resolve to uphold the most deeply held principles of our societies and to defeat those who would *impose their fanaticism and extremism on all of us.*"

Former Secretary of State Henry A. Kissinger made an observation in an article published in June 2007, which revealed another possible motive. She may be a part of a grand game Islamic fundamentalist domino that would be a bigger disaster for America and the free world than losing the Vietnam War. "Defeat in Vietnam had long-term psychological significance for countries that relied on America for their defense. A collapse in Iraq would immediately weaken societies with significant Muslim populations, as radical Islam gained momentum from Indonesia, through India, to North Africa and Western Europe," he wrote.

Mr. Kissinger's discovery is not new. It might have been inspired by a statement President Bush made a few years ago although the former Secretary of State toned it down somewhat. In Oct. 2005, President

Bush declared that the Islamic extremist had a universal motive. They want to establish *a radical Islamic empire that spans from Spain to Indonesia.* In his speech at the National Endowment for Democracy on October 6, 2005, President Bush asserted: "The militants believe that controlling one country will rally the Muslim masses, enabling them to overthrow all moderate governments in the region, and establish a radical Islamic empire that spans from Spain to Indonesia."

If none of the above is correct, we still wouldn't run out of characterizations and motives to label Sajida al-Rishawi. Thanks to the Bush administration's abundant creativity, we can give her a one-size-fits-all label for terrorists: *murderous ideologist.* In the speech given at the National Endowment for Democracy noted above, President Bush also said: "*The murderous ideology of the Islamic radicals is the great challenge of our new century,*" (Tom Raum, AP).

Had Sajida al-Rishawi succeeded in blowing herself up we would know her as one of those peculiar human beings, who hate freedom or cannot stand the thought of a peaceful and free Iraq or abhor the Westerners' way of life or want to impose fanaticism and extremism on everybody in the world or want to establish a radical Islamic empire that spans from Spain to Indonesia. But she failed and lived to face Jordanian investigators and justice. And from this, we discovered her true motive. She said that she just wanted to avenge the deaths of her three brothers, who had been killed in conflict with U.S.-led forces in Fallujah.

As Commander-in-Chief, you should be aware of this not-on-the-list, newly born kind of terrorist and think of a strategy to prevent it from growing.

The good news is there aren't many Iraqi sisters who react violently to their brothers' killers like this one. Woman suicide bombers are rare, especially among those sisters who are mourning the loss of their brothers.

The bad news is that any victim of an enemy's killing creates a brotherly or sisterly relationship with an unknown number of total strangers.

Many men, and women, too, instinctively feel the need to avenge the deaths of sisters or brothers they never met. It doesn't only happen in Iraq. After 9/11, millions of Americans supported their President's war against terrorists who killed three thousand people whose relationship with them is only "fellow American citizen". Many American soldiers interviewed said they were willing to fight in Iraq or Afghanistan to protect their country and to avenge the deaths of American brothers, sisters, fathers, sons, daughters... they didn't even know the names.

The more killings, that happen intentionally or unintentionally, the greater the number of this brand-new kind of terrorist emerged.

And occupation creates a rich ground and perfect climate for it to grow, since the longer the occupation lasts the more such unavoidable killings will occur.

17

LOVING THEIR CHILDREN

Testifying before the Senate Armed Services Committee on Aug. 3, 2006, the nominee Chairman of the Joint Chiefs of Staff, Gen. Peter Pace, predicted the future of the Iraq war by concluding that only love would bring peace to that country. *"The violence in Iraq will only subside once Iraqis begin loving their children more than they hate their enemy,"* he said.

Less than ten days later, on the way to Iraq, Gen. Pace similarly advised the Iraqi people on how to solve their deadly conflict. *"The Shiite and Sunni leaders are going to have to love their kids more than they hate each other, so they can go about building their country,"* he told reporters.

If Gen. Pace is correct, all the U.S. military's strategies and tactics up to now have been terribly misguided, and useless in pacifying Iraq. An invasion, occupation and even some temporary "surges" cannot make the Iraqis love their children more. Instead they have pumped up their hatred.

Should we solve the Iraq war by withdrawing our troops to reduce the source of much of the hatred, and send to Iraq brigades of educators, philosophers, psychologists, poets, Dr. Phil, etc... to make Iraqis love more than hate?

I'm afraid no human powers are capable of performing that miracle on all the Iraqis, or at least, millions of Iraqi parents. Only Almighty God can plant the seed of love into human hearts in such big scale.

But we don't have to worry about performing God's work. Gen. Pace isn't right. His remarks do not reflect the true state of mind of the Iraqi people. The only practical value of his statement is to unintentionally send a gentle insult to Iraqi parents, especially those fathers who are primarily involved in violent acts.

I believe Iraqi fathers love their children no less than Joe Johnson, an American, loves his son.

Mr. Johnson's son, Justin, 22, was killed by a roadside bomb in Baghdad, in April 2004. One year later, Cpl. Johnson joined his Georgia National Guard unit and headed to Iraq to seek revenge.
For more than a year, Johnson fought to follow in his son's footsteps to Iraq. There was a sense of soldierly duty, but what most drew him here was his desire for vengeance.
"I can shoot an insurgent and not lose a bit of sleep over it," said Johnson, a home builder from Lyerly, Ga. "I think any father would feel a sense of revenge. To me, it would be like someone down the street killed my son and I sat by and didn't do anything about it." (Jeremy Redmon and Ron Martz of Cox News Service, October 11, 2005)
Out of love for his son, an American father sought revenge for his son's death, engaging in violent acts of war. I would never dare to say that he loves his son less than he hates something else in the world.
Mr. Johnson's son was a soldier, and was killed while performing his duty. The Iraqis' sons and daughters, who are being destroyed by bullets and bombs of terrorists or U.S. forces, are mostly young children. A great number of the unfortunate Iraqi parents would feel the same painful thought as Joe Johnson: *"It would be like someone down the street killed my son..."* and they couldn't just sit by, rather they want to do something about it.
The Iraqi fathers, who still have their children alive and uninjured, also cannot just "sit by." They have to fight enemies to protect their children before the fighting becomes an act of revenge.

A Sunni father, for example, sees not only the safety of his children at stake, but also their future. For years, his enemies have been trying hard to rob the Sunni people of their livelihood and a share of country's wealth.

The insurgent forces, born after the invasion, have drastically grown following L. Paul Bremer's de-Baathification program and the order to disband Iraqi army. Since most of the army are Sunni Muslims, Sunni population fall under suspicion and became targets of the occupation forces. When President Bush's democracy gave the Iraqi government an overwhelming Shiite majority with close ties to Iran, the Sunnis had to confront a much more formidable adversary. Prisons in Iraq were full of Sunni men. The tortured bodies of Sunnis were exposed by the dozen every day. Sunni women and children made up the lion's share of civilian deaths by the U.S. military's stray bullets and errant bombs. The newly installed Iraqi Parliament also fashioned a Constitution that robs Sunnis of their share of government jobs and of the country's oil resources. Loving his children becomes one of the motives that instigate a Sunni father to sacrifice his life fighting to protect their lives and future.

The violence in Iraq subsided after the "surge," when Gen. David H. Petraeus was wise enough to arm and pay about ninety thousand "awakening" Sunni militants, who protect the Sunni population, thereby giving them some hope for the future.

From the perspective of a Shiite father, the picture is less dark, but still far from rosy. As victims of Saddam Hussein's dictatorship, the Shiites were actually liberated by and became allies of the U.S.-led occupation. Backed up by U.S. forces and holding a majority of the nation's population, allowing them to dominate elections, Shiite leaders become leaders of the country. They created a Constitution, laws, rules, regulations that benefit the Shiites. No doubt the Shiites will have a bright future. But until then, ordinary Shiite people have to deal with angry, desperate Sunnis who have joined the insurgency or Al Qeada. They have children murdered by terrorists who need to be avenged and the living ones who need to be protected.

The Iraqi fathers, Sunni or Shiite, have chosen to fight to the death because they love their children *and* hate their enemy. Hatred is the other side of the equation, not the weight of the opposite side of the scale, which would balance and cancel the effect of love.

President Bush should be concerned when one of his top generals, instead providing the public with a valid assessment of the state of Iraq war and a promising military strategy to deal with it, produces instead a psychological analysis, which dismisses the degree of love Iraqi parents have for their children.

Whoever as Commander-in-Chief falls into Mr. Bush's situation should immediately advise all his military leaders to respect and never underestimate the love of a father and mother, no matter what country they live in.

*

*   *

General Pace's words remind me of a story I heard about 40 years ago. During World War II, a German soldier also underestimated the love of a father for his son from the enemy side. Unlike General Pace's, however, his mistake only lasted a few seconds.

The story was related by a staff writer for *Back Khoa* magazine. We had gathered for a meeting to discuss current events and literary affairs when he brought it up. I did not have a chance to read it for myself, but, as I recall, it seemed to be a war memoir or piece of short fiction by a writer from Eastern Europe. To the best of my recollection, it went something like this:

One morning during the war, a German soldier, the only one in his unit fluent in the local language of the occupied area, was assigned to take two captured spies to the field behind the encampment and carry out their executions.

The two condemned were a farmer and his son, a sixteen-year-old boy. Both had been captured the previous evening while wandering about on the hill near the German base. After hours of intense interrogation, the commander concluded that they were spies from the local resistance and ordered that they be executed the next morning.

Our German soldier, having served as the interpreter during the interrogation was chosen on the spot by his superior to carry out the executions, a task he did not particularly relish. Unlike some of his comrades in arms, he'd rather use his firearm only in battle.

As they left the camp, the condemned father and son walked slowly, even though they weren't tied up or blindfolded, because the terrain was densely covered with thorny brushes and knee-high, sharp-edged and stiff weeds. Our soldier followed them, somewhat impatient, but feeling no need to order them to quicken their pace. Having listened to the details of the man's life, his family, his daily routine, during the interrogations, he felt a certain empathy toward the two, and this prevented him from acting harshly. He thought to himself that perhaps the father and son were not even aware they were about to be shot.

Upon arriving at a place where the thorny brushes were even denser and the knife-like weeds taller, the boy hesitated, reluctant to go on. "Let's stop. We'll be fine here." said the soldier. The father and son stopped, turned around, and looked at him, puzzled.

"They really don't know." thought the soldier. A twinge of pity came then passed. Cocking his rifle, he said in a slow, measured voice, "Both of you are condemned to be shot for being spies." In his own way, he was hoping they would make his job a little easier by running, so he could pick them off like a hunter.

But the two remained motionless. The boy kept his head down while the father stared vacantly in front of him, perhaps exhausted from the beating and interrogation of the night before.

The soldier raised his rifle. Then, reluctantly, he lowered it. "I can only fire one round at a time. Which one of you wants to die last?" he asked, still hoping…

The father suddenly became alert and animated. He frantically begged the soldier, "Let me die last, please! I want to die last! Take him first! Please!"

Our German soldier was utterly shocked at this outburst. "How intense is man's instinct for survival! And it's only for a few seconds!" he thought. At the same time, the desperate, cowardly plea for survival from the father greatly disturbed him. Enraged, he aimed his rifle at the boy and pulled the trigger.

At the crack of the gunshot, the father jerked forward to catch his falling child. He lifted the wounded boy in his arms and very slowly, very gently laid the lifeless body on a spot of bare ground.

And so, with his own life about to be ended, the father had decided to use his last moments of existence to soften the fall of his child, away from thorns and sharp blades of weeds.

18

PRESIDENTIAL ADVISORY STAFF

My last advice: put all your effort and devote your heart and mind into selecting right people for the Presidential Advisory Staff. And you should pray for you never have any adviser who is as ignorant and incompetent as some people in the President Bush's entourage.

In the years since the Iraq invasion began, many of the world's Commanders-in-Chief– ours included – are still confused and struggling to identify the motive of the terrorists. However, only six months after the fall of Baghdad, one member of the U.S. Army accurately detected the real identity and main goal of majority of the insurgents.

In October 2003, Lt. Col. Kim Keslung, an orthopedic surgeon of the U.S. Army's 21st Combat Support Hospital, was working hard in a tent hospital. This tent was one of four such U.S. facilities in Iraq, and located deep in the so-called Sunni Triangle north and west of Baghdad. At that time, all four had to deal with the *biggest influx of military casualties since the Vietnam War.*

Yaroslav Trofimov, a reporter for the *Wall Street Journal,* described an event that happened one day in the life of the surgeon:

BALAD, Iraq -- Shortly after 11 a.m. last Thursday, the crackle of the radio brought the first of the day's bad news to the U.S. Army's 21st Combat Support Hospital.

"Two U.S. soldiers injured," a helicopter pilot said on the radio. "Six minutes to landing." An armored ambulance Humvee rushed to the nearby landing pad.

As the chopper's blades churned up sand and dust near the field hospital, the ambulance driver and the pilots unloaded a stretcher carrying the more severely injured soldier and ran back to the Humvee. Sgt. Chuck Bartels, a reservist, was still clear-headed despite his injuries. His face was bloody and swollen, one of his arms was a mess of torn flesh.

... The emergency room was an air-conditioned tent decorated with Halloween skeletons and drawings mailed by children from the U.S. Doctors and nurses quickly converged on Sgt. Bartels, 25 years old, and his injured buddy, Sgt. Jared Myers, 23.

... After the emergency room, Sgt. Bartels was wheeled into the operating room. His buddy, Sgt. Myers, who received shrapnel wounds in his right arm and face, called his family back in Kansas as he waited to be treated. The two sergeants, reservists attached to the Fourth Infantry Division, were driving from a meeting at the town of Baqouba's agriculture ministry office. They accompanied a civil-affairs officer, Capt. John Teal, who was filling in for their usual captain, on leave in the U.S.

Sgt. Myers asked nurses what happened to Capt. Teal. No one could muster the courage to tell the sergeant the captain was dead, instantly killed by the roadside bomb that went through their unarmored Humvee.

After Sgt. Bartels' surgery was over, he was wheeled into an intensive-care tent and put on a cot next to an 8-year-old Iraqi girl being treated for massive burns. A large, muscular man, the sergeant was called up just as he was finishing his work for a master's degree in Russian studies at the University of Kansas. The operation had left his right arm just a short bandaged stump. Pieces of flesh were missing from his face.

Trofimov managed to get a quick interview with the surgeon who cared for Sgt. Bartels. In just a few sentences, Dr. Keslung offered him deep insight into the core reasons for the current influx of violence:

The orthopedic surgeon, Lt. Col. Kim Keslung, sat down after the surgery and sipped Kool-Aid. Her desert-tan uniform was stained with blood. "His nerves and blood vessels were just shredded. There wasn't anything to fix in his arm," she said. "He'll have to adjust to his new life."

*... It was a mistake to discount the Iraqi resistance, Col. Keslung said, adding, "**If someone invaded Texas, we'd do the same thing**."*

At almost the same time as Trofimov's report was published, in Oct. 2003, Paul Bremer was called back to the White House to inform the President about the situation in Iraq and the identity and motives of the insurgents. His report compelled President Bush to give a cheerful Rose Garden news Conference where Bremer said that many wonderful things had happened in Iraq, and Mr. Bush told the whole world that the insurgents are simply a bunch of people "who can't stand the thought of a free and peaceful Iraq," as mentioned in chapter 16.

Dr. Keslung clearly saw the insurgents as decent human beings who reacted to invaders and occupiers exactly as Americans would if the latter found themselves in the same situation. But our President, based on information and suggestion from Ambassador Bremer, tried to sell the American people and the world his new discovery: the existence of an abnormal human race consisting of brain-dead zombies who were willing to fight the occupiers to death because they want to deny freedom to their fellow citizens and peace to their country.

Ambassador Bremer is not the only one to blame. Apparently, no one in the Bush advisory staff – including that strategic genius Karl Rove – was capable of detecting any thing strange in his report or absurd in the President's statement.

As Commander - in - Chief, you should try your best to have advisers who at least possess common knowledge about human nature, like Dr. Kim Keslung.

The skill of someone like Lt. Col. Keslung can heal an American's wounds. But a presidential adviser with Keslung's intelligence and common sense can help you make right decisions, policies, and strategies to prevent Americans' blood from spilling unnecessarily on the desert sands.